DISRAELI'S FICTION

DISRAELI'S FICTION

Daniel R. Schwarz
Associate Professor and Director of Undergraduate Studies
Department of English
Cornell University

First published 1979 by
THE MACMILLAN PRESS LTD
Associated companies in Delhi
Dublin Hong Kong Johannesburg Lagos
Melbourne New York Singapore Tokyo

Printed in Great Britain by
Billings and Sons Ltd
Guildford, London and Worcester

British Library Cataloguing in Publication Data

Schwarz, Daniel R.
Disraeli's fiction
1. Disraeli, Benjamin, *Earl of Beaconsfield* – Criticism and interpretation
I. Title
823'.8 PR4087

ISBN 0–333–26818–0

Contents

Acknowledgements

I wish to thank Dr Park Honan for his invaluable suggestions and encouragement. Professor Ian Gregor, my mentor and friend, has taught me the meaning of humane teaching and scholarship. I am obligated to my colleagues and students at Cornell for an exciting intellectual atmosphere in which to think, learn, write and teach.

I appreciate grants from the Center of International Studies of Cornell University and the Cornell Humanities Faculty Research Fund. The National Trust, which maintains the Disraeli Archives at Hughenden, has graciously given me permission to quote from the Disraeli papers. Portions of Chapter 3 appeared in *Victorian Newsletter* (Spring 1975) and an earlier version of Chapter 4 appeared in *The Journal of Narrative Technique* (January, 1974). I am grateful to their editors for allowing me to use this material.

DANIEL R. SCHWARZ

Cornell University
Ithaca, New York
January 1979

For my wife Marcia

Introduction

In the National Portrait Gallery in London, there are two quite different pictures of Benjamin Disraeli (1804–81). The first, an engraving by H. Robinson after an 1840 painting by A. E. Chalon, shows Disraeli with long, somewhat unkempt hair, an arrogant look approaching a sneer on his lips, inflamed eyes as if he had been up all night, a sloppy, creased coat, and an open shirt, his neck hardly concealed by a cravat. He cuts a most unconventional figure for a public man, and his mysterious, yet audacious air is emphasised by the fact that we cannot see his hands. In the second portrait, flatteringly painted by Sir John Everett Millais in 1881, the last year of Disraeli's life, the former Prime Minister, in formal dress and bow tie with arms folded, is the picture of propriety. Looking very much younger than his years, confident and poised, with arms folded, neat, stern without being unduly severe, and clearly in complete control of his emotions, he is the embodiment of the successful statesman. His taut self-control and his polished manner (every hair of beard and head is in place) contrast so strikingly with the earlier portrait that it reminds us that Disraeli, more than most men, consciously created the public self that stares so imposingly at us. Yet Disraeli never quite succeeded in erasing from the public mind the portrait of the younger Disraeli, the man whose novels and behaviour scandalised England. Not without a touch of anti-Semitism, critics twitted Disraeli about his transformation. For example, the caption accompanying the first cartoon (by C. Pellegrini) ever to appear in *Vanity Fair* (1869) read: 'He educated the Tories and dished the Whigs to pass Reform, but to have become what he is from what he was is the greatest Reform of all'. Similarly, a cartoon in *Punch* on 29 January 1867 comments on Disraeli's delicate footwork during the passage of the Second Reform Bill.

In the following chapters, I shall be concerned with Disraeli's career as a novelist. Were his novels not important as works of art, they would be worth studying for what they tell us about one of the major figures of the nineteenth century. Taken as a whole these novels are a considerable artistic achievement and, if both quality and output are taken into account, need yield only to the works of Austen, Dickens, Thackeray, Eliot, Trollope, Hardy and maybe Scott among nineteenth-century novelists. At the university where I teach, my enthusiasm for Disraeli's novels is regarded as a tolerable critical eccentricity, because I teach and write about 'major' novelists. Yet when I prevail upon students or colleagues to read *Sybil*, they are invariably enthusiastic. Nor does their excitement diminish after reading *Coningsby* or *Vivian Grey*; indeed their appetite is whetted for more, and they continue to enjoy subsequent novels, including some like *Lothair* and *Henrietta Temple* that have been read infrequently since the nineteenth century.

In this era of literary criticism, when attention is paid to minor writers whose work provides projects for dissertations but gives scant pleasure to anyone, it seems odd that Disraeli has been ignored. Richard A. Levine's *Benjamin Disraeli* (New York: Twayne, 1968), the only book-length critical study of Disraeli's novels, was published almost a decade ago. Levine does not give serious attention to the entire canon. Rather he focuses on the Young England trilogy (*Coningsby*, *Sybil* and *Tancred*) and discusses the other novels in relation to the trilogy and Disraeli's later ideas. I shall be much more concerned than he with the aesthetics of Disraeli's novels and with the relation between Disraeli's novels and his life.[1] A. B. Walkley's remark in 1922 is still appropriate: 'Disraeli's novels are documents as well as delights. It is a perpetual marvel to me that so few people . . . seem to read them.'[2] Disraeli's novels merit renewed attention not only because of their wit, insight, breadth, and vision and because they reveal the consciousness of one of the Victorian giants at crucial stages in his career, but also because they present strikingly original imagined worlds. In common with the other great Victorian novels, Disraeli's fictional works have the capacity to tell us something about another age and about ourselves. Like the major Victorian novelists, Disraeli is a deft psychologist and a student of the manners and mores of his time, but his political career gives him a unique perspective.

Disraeli's literary career spans over half a century, from 1826 to 1880. He published the first volumes of *Vivian Grey* when Scott, Blake, Wordsworth and Coleridge were still alive and before any of the major Victorians, excepting Carlyle, were published. He concluded his career in 1880, a year when Dickens and Thackeray were dead and George Eliot was to die, and Thomas Hardy had already published *Far From the Madding Crowd* and *The Return of the Native*.

Disraeli tells us something about the history of taste in the nineteenth century. His early novels – *Vivian Grey* (1826–7), *The Young Duke* (1831), *Contarini Fleming* (1832) and *Alroy* (1833) – met the middle-class desire for revelations of aristocratic life, for romances about bizarre characters in strange lands, and for extreme behaviour on the part of wilful egoists posing as latter-day Byrons. As an outsider, as a man who savoured his own feelings and sought unusual sensations, the youthful Disraeli saw himself as an heir to Byron and Shelley. But in the later 1830s Disraeli, like Dickens, responded to audiences who wanted sentiment and sweetness; in *Henrietta Temple* Disraeli wrote about love between virginal young women and idealistic young men whose motives are temporarily misunderstood because of circumstances beyond their control. Even when he wrote of Byron and Shelley in *Venetia*, he threw the mantle of Victorian respectability over them in spite of his empathy with their unconventionality. In the late 1840s, he met the demand for serious novels that addressed themselves to major moral and political ideas. In *Lothair* (1870) he drew upon the public's fascination – rekindled by the conversion of the Marquess of Bute – with the journey from Anglicanism to Roman Catholicism, while in *Endymion* (1880) he responded to the interest in character psychology created by Browning, Eliot and Hardy, which was really part of an inward turning and questioning as the Victorian era passed its high tide of confidence. Throughout his career his fiction fulfilled the nineteenth-century fascination with heroic men; this fascination reflected a need for larger-than-life personalities in an age of uncertainty.

Lord David Cecil once remarked: 'Disraeli's novels are not strictly speaking novels. . . . but discussions on political and religious questions put into fictional form.'[3] While Cecil probably had in mind, among other things, the treatment of the Chartist movement and Catholicism in *Sybil*, nothing is further from the truth. In all his novels, Disraeli revelled in the infinite variety of human personality and enjoyed setting major and minor characters in motion in a dramatic situation for the sheer joy of hypothesising how they would behave. Young Disraeli particularly admired independent people who, like himself, had dashing, dynamic, and idiosyncratic personalities. He wished to experience every conceivable emotion and play every possible role. Thus, in his art, he experimented with kinds of mimesis, ranging from cartoons and stereotypes to psychological realism. He tested a wide range of styles and voices; and even when he was not entirely successful, as in the union of prose and poetry in

Alroy, we are not sorry he made the attempt. Just as Disraeli tested and discarded a number of political positions as he sought his public role, so as an artist he experimented with a variety of styles and wrote in a multitude of genres. He wrote Silver Fork novels (*Vivian Grey, The Young Duke*), *Bildungsromane* (*Coningsby* and *Lothair*), a satiric imaginary voyage (*Popanilla*), a *Künstlerroman* (*Contarini Fleming*), a novel of purpose (*Sybil*), an historical romance (*Alroy*), and an historical reminiscence (*Endymion*). In *Coningsby* and *Sybil*, he virtually invented the genre of the political novel in English.

To the reader accustomed to novels constructed upon recurring images and mythic parallels, to novels in which the verbal texture is the crucial ingredient of organisation, Disraeli's novels will seem even more loose and unwieldy than the longer novels of Dickens or Eliot. Disraeli's novels are not tightly woven prose poems, but spacious forms in which the author's eye and mind have room to move about. While we read Joyce, Nabokov or Kafka, our attention is focused on every detail because we know that the only possibility of understanding what we are reading depends upon thinking reflectively about the significance of every word. Reading Disraeli's novels is not that kind of experience. It is more like moving from room to room in a large museum than studying a single painting for hours. The ample length of his novels gives him space to digress when he feels the urge and to develop his characters over a period of years. Despite his penchant for the epigrammatic sentence, Disraeli's unit is not the sentence or even the paragraph, but the dramatic episode. Although his 1840s work focused more upon theme, Disraeli conceived his novels primarily in terms of a central character who is tested by crucial episodes. This is true whether he creates versions of himself or whether he is exploring secondary figures. His imagination functions most effectively when it is engaged by dramatic scenes, particularly those that have a strong visual component: the Young Duke in the gambling den, Lothair's visitation by Theodora's ghost, Coningsby's bold refusal to run for office at Lord Monmouth's behest, the woman and children at Diggs' tommy-shop.

Disraeli's novels have been frequently misinterpreted by readers who do not understand the way Disraeli's imagination works. For example, John Holloway in his splendid chapter in *The Victorian Sage* has complained: 'The novels rarely develop through any internal logic: they turn on casual events, on delightful and exhilarating operations of chance'.[4] As we shall see, the logic of the first four novels is directed by the moods and values of their creator, and depends not on the separation of author from text, but on the felt presence of the author within the text. If, in a sense, Disraeli at times competes with his characters for his reader's attention, this sets up a fruitful tension. Until the political trilogy, Disraeli's protagonist is usually the outlet for his unique fantasies and passions, while the narrator is usually the objectification of his conscience – his social and moral self – which censors his atavistic energy and impulses. The exuberance of Disraeli's early style cannot fully mask its tendency to pleonasm and pomposity. As he matures, however, he learns to use his style to reflect the psyche of the characters he is describing and, when he wishes, to step aside and comment ironically on that character's thought processes. Yet, until the trilogy, Disraeli does not submerge his personality and, like a puppeteer on stage, deflects attention from his characters to his own often dominant presence.

His novels alternate between realistic depictions of the nineteenth century and illuminating distortions of that period's manners, morals and politics. As a profound student of human psychology, Disraeli takes his place in the tradition of Richardson, Austen and Eliot, those English novelists who observe human behaviour in terms of manners and social conditions. But his eye for the grotesque and his taste for the fantastic place him in the tradition of Fielding, Dickens and Sterne. Whether he uses wonderfully extravagant plots and flamboyant self-dramatising narrators, as in the early novels, or the baroque plots and more controlled speakers of the later novels, the heroic quest of the major figure is the organising principle of all his novels.

Disraeli's career as a novelist gives an important if partial insight into his elusive but evolving personality and character. His novels are imagined worlds that reflect and parody aspects of nineteenth-century life, but they are also the psychic and linguistic gestures of a major historical figure. It was while considering Disraeli that Sir Isaiah Berlin wrote: 'A man may not be sincere in his political speeches or his letters, but his works of art are of himself and tell one where his true values lie'.[5] Reading his novels we read the biography of Disraeli's soul. Particularly in the period between 1826 and 1836, the novels are his most revealing *actions* in the sense that they most accurately reflect his doubts and anxieties, his hopes and aspirations. In the novels, Disraeli presented various aspects of his complicated personality as he imagined it at a particular time and place; the novels stand as vehicles for which his mind and psyche are the tenors. Coexisting within the novels are conflicting aspects of Disraeli's character: Disraeli the stern moralist and Disraeli the optimist; Disraeli the imaginative man seeking refuge in his fantasies and Disraeli the pragmatist; Disraeli the private man who enjoys introspective moments, and Disraeli the public figure who hides his emotions beneath a façade of nonchalance. The figure that emerges is not only multidimensional and complex, but almost larger than life. Disraeli as an artist not only captures our imagination because he is a major political figure, but because we recognise, as did his contemporaries, that he was one of the remarkable figures of his era.

As a literary critic, I wish to complement the research of political scientists, historians and biographers. I have tried to strike a balance between reading the texts for their aesthetic values, and reading the texts for what they show us about Disraeli. I shall discuss the fascinating relationship between the novels and Disraeli the historic figure, and show how his novel writing played an important role in shaping his character. While I often place Disraeli's fiction in the context of his life and the nineteenth-century milieu, my focus is on the full-length novels. I have omitted the poems, the fragment *Falconet*, and other minor works which add little to our understanding of Disraeli the artist or Disraeli the public figure.

1 Metaphors of The Self: Disraeli's Early Fiction

I

Describing the process of writing *Death in Venice*, Thomas Mann recalled, 'Originally the tale was to be brief and modest. But things or whatever better word there may be for the conception *organic* have a will of their own, and shape themselves accordingly. . . . The truth is that every piece of work is a realization, fragmentary but complete in itself, of our individuality; and this kind of realization is the sole and painful way we have of getting the particular experience – no wonder, then, that the process is attended by surprises.'[1] Mann reminds us that the author both creates a text and discovers an aspect of his or her self during its creation. In Disraeli's first four novels – *Vivian Grey* (1826–27), *The Young Duke* (1831), *Contarini Fleming* (1832) and *The Wondrous Tale of Alroy* (1833), he 'realized' aspects of his individuality. Not only did he create imagined worlds in his novels, but the novels played a crucial role in creating his character and personality. In discussing Disraeli's first four novels, I shall argue that understanding the symbiotic relationship between author and text is an essential condition to appreciating his art. An 1833 entry in Disraeli's 'mutilated' diary shows that the novels compensate for his failure to excel even as they protest against accepted English conventions and manners:

> The world calls me 'conceited' – The world is in error. I trace all the blunders of my life to sacrificing my own opinion to that of others. When I was considered very conceited *indeed*, I was nervous, and had self-confidence only by fits. I intend in future to act entirely from my own impulse. I have an unerring instinct. I can read characters at a glance; few men can deceive me. My mind is a continental mind. It is a revolutionary mind. I am only truly great in action. If ever I am placed in a truly eminent position I shall

> prove this. I could rule the House of Commons, although there would be a great prejudice against me at first. It is the most jealous assembly in the world. The fine character of our English society, the consequences of our aristocratic institutions, renders a *career* difficult.[2]

The subsequent passage in the diary makes it clear that literature is a compensation for the frustration he feels at not being given the opportunity to play a major role in public events: 'Poetry is the safety valve of my passions – but I wish to *act* what I *write*. My works are the embodification of my feelings. In *Vivian Grey* I have portrayed my active and real ambition: In *Alroy* my ideal ambition: [*Contarini Fleming: A Psychological Romance*] is a development of my poetic character. This trilogy is the secret history of my feelings – I shall write no more about myself.'

II

Vivian Grey is about the precocious and ambitious title character's efforts to attain political influence through Machiavellian manœuvres that ultimately fail. If Vivian portrays Disraeli's 'active and real ambition', it was because Disraeli recognised that one aspect of himself savoured power for its own sake. Vivian's sensational and erratic school career has striking parallels to Disraeli's. Vivian's dependence on the co-operation of others reflects Disraeli's own view, in 1826, that a man without wealth, family and power required help to rise to a position of responsibility. Despite his father's cultivation and tolerance, Vivian becomes an arrogant, condescending, proud and, at times, violent young man. Convinced that he is adept at managing and manipulating people for his own ends, Vivian urges the disappointed and sulking Marquess of Carabas to form a political party. The proposed party requires a leader, and Vivian, the ever resourceful master of *Realpolitik*, decides that the one man who would give the project respectability is the Marquess's enemy, John Cleveland. Vivian's mission to win Cleveland mirrors Disraeli's own effort to convince Lockhart, Scott's son-in-law, to manage a daily paper, *The Representative*, that he was founding.[3] Just as *The Representative* collapsed, so does the political project. But Vivian is betrayed by the friends upon whom he depends, principally Mrs Felix Lorraine, the sister-in-law of the Marquess of Carabas, the former minister with whom Vivian enters into an alliance. Cleveland holds Vivian responsible for the collapse and challenges him to a duel with pistols. Vivian kills Cleveland, and after an illness attributable to a stricken conscience, he finally leaves England. For all his energy and intelligence, it is hard to imagine what Vivian could have done to arrest his headlong rush to destruction once he committed himself to the political intrigue. Nothing would have forestalled Mrs Lorraine's pathological behaviour.

Published anonymously when Disraeli was twenty-one, the first four books were a sensation, and keys were published matching fictional characters to the supposed models. Writing of Vivian's renunciation and despair in 1826 enabled Disraeli to cope with his self-doubts and melancholy that resulted from the failure of *The Representative*. Once these doubts were encapsulated within an objective form – the work of fiction – he cast off some of the gloom and was ready to return to the world of action. It is characteristic of the relationship between fiction and life in Disraeli's career that as soon as the original four volumes were completed, he began a grand tour. Thus, the resigned maturity that Disraeli attributes to Vivian in the later books was only a temporary resting place for himself.

In 1827 Disraeli wrote four additional books as a sequel to capitalise on the interest aroused by the original books which purported to expose incompetent and scandalous behaviour. If these books have been patronised far more than they deserve, that is in part because the 1853 edition, the text that most readers know, expurgates some of the liveliest passages from the original 1826–7 edition. Vivian has now renounced ambition, and in Book V, the first of the 1827 books, Violet Fane, the one woman he loves, dies. The rest of the sequel is a travelogue in which Vivian is used as a means of exposing the follies of continental customs and, implicitly, of showing England in a far gentler light than the original four books. Vivian becomes a rather passive Gulliver figure who encounters a series of bizarre adventures. After Violet Fane's death, Vivian plays Don Quixote to Esper George's Sancho Panza. By the novel's end, the Machiavellian political manœuvrer of the early sections has become a melancholy idealist. The most important figure in these books in terms of Disraeli's psyche and political development is Beckendorff, whose worldliness, guile, use of power, and political ingenuity fascinate Vivian and, as the narrator reveals, Disraeli. Beckendorff is another version of Disraeli's 'real ambition'. That Beckendorff has pulled himself from common origins to a position of great influence shows the persistent attraction of the political Cinderella myth to Disraeli, despite his own disappointment and that of Vivian Grey, the fictional character through whom he dramatises that disappointment. By the time he had written the sequel Disraeli had put behind him the gloom resulting from his abortive efforts to form a daily newspaper, *The Representative*. He no longer viewed the ambitious man as a victim of circumstances.

The original and sequel of *Vivian Grey* form a novel composed of three sections: the rise and fall of Vivian as a political figure which occupies the first four books; the abortive love affair with Violet Fane which occupies Book V; and the three travel volumes, Books VI to VIII, where he is more an observer of manners than an involved, three-dimensional character. After the first four books, except for the two unfortunate love affairs, Vivian's emotional life is really a secondary concern.

Although in the first four books Vivian is a character who has an inflated view of himself and whose behaviour seems excessive and bizarre, Disraeli's condemnation is nevertheless mixed with sympathy. Disraeli does empathise with him, particularly in his moments of self-doubt and frustration. While Disraeli shows that Vivian's ambition and pride are responsible for his fall, he is kindly disposed to him not only in his subsequent travels, but even in the English chapters. Although Vivian is a consummate egoist, he is usually a good-natured rogue in the picaro tradition whom Disraeli uses to expose the artificiality and pretensions of the aristocracy. Disraeli mitigates our harsh judgment by showing how Vivian intervenes on behalf of his friend John Conyers. He also demonstrates that despite Vivian's apparent shrewdness he is no match for Mrs Felix Lorraine in Machiavellian behaviour nor for Carabas in self-interested hypocrisy. For most of the people whom he gets the better of behave even more selfishly than he does. Despite his vow to be more unscrupulous than the most unscrupulous, he is outwitted by his adversaries, and his killing of Cleveland results from a shot that was meant to miss. Often when he poses as an expert in manipulating others, he is revealed as a gull deserving of our sympathy.

Like *Vanity Fair*, which it may have influenced despite Thackeray's and Disraeli's enmity, *Vivian Grey* is a Book of Vices that ominously warns of the consequences of various kinds of pernicious behaviour. The original four books published in 1826 address the vice of intellectual arrogance. Of Vivian, the narrator remarks, 'It has been shown that he was one precociously convinced of the necessity of managing mankind, by studying their tempers and humouring their weaknesses' (III, i, p. 89).[4] But the demise of Vivian's plans teaches him the folly of trying to manage mankind and of allowing ambition to subsume one's private identity. The later books combine the genres of the picaro tale and the imaginary voyage. Vivian, experienced and morally mature, observes folly and vice. His vantage point is that of one who has learned the lesson of *Ecclesiastes*: 'To wake from your bright hopes, and feel that all is vanity, to be roused from your crafty plans and know that all is worthless, is a bitter, but your sure, destiny' (V, i, p. 165). Once Vivian reforms and begins his travels, Disraeli uses his perspective to support the narrator's satire of other vices. Book V deals with gambling as a form of dissipation; Book VI, i addresses excessive and pointless drinking; Book VI, iii focuses on the folly of political intrigue and the struggle for pomp and power in Little Lilliput, and implicitly holds up an ironic mirror to Vivian's pursuit of power in the first four books; Book VII, ii satirises another kind of Vanity, that of the world of fashion where the silliest garb and a fool such as Von Aslingen, who has the audacity to wear it, are honoured. Book VII, iii exposes the intellectual pretensions of philosophers and literary critics; Book VII, viii mocks military behaviour; and Book VII, ix satirises the pretensions and wasted energy of fancy dress balls.

Beckendorff, the major figure in Books VI and VII, has a philosophy that Disraeli himself might have articulated at most stages of his career. 'A man's fate is his own temper; and according to that will be his opinion as to the particular manner in which the course of events is regulated. A consistent man believes in Destiny, a capricious man in Chance. . . . Man is not the creature of circumstances. Circumstances are the creatures of men. We are free agents, and man is more powerful than matter. I recognize no intervening influence between that of the established course of nature and my own mind' (VI, vii, pp. 368–9). Beckendorff believes a man may shape his own destiny by the sheer force of his will and personality. Beckendorff is the successful version of the egoistic alternative that Vivian, but not his creator, had put behind him. While the melancholy, disillusioned Grey sees Beckendorff's philosophy as a version of the false principles he once held, Disraeli's narrative voice is impatient with Vivian's ennui and is sympathetic with the bold, idiosyncratic minister. Disraeli never really endorses the passivity and resignation of Vivian who recalls the undeserved loss of Violet whom he had loved 'with passions subdued, and . . . a mind matured.' (VI, vii, p. 370).

Dramatizing an idea in fiction often helped Disraeli clarify it for himself. Thus in 1833 he wrote in a defensive but significant campaign pamphlet entitled *What is He? by the Author of Vivian Grey*, 'Let us not forget also an influence too much underrated in this age of bustling mediocrity – the influence of individual character'.[5] Disraeli's belief that man's character determines his fate, and that man can control his life, enabled him to overcome unfavourable circumstances and setbacks at every stage of his career. He believed that the ability to shape events *determines* one's capacity for leadership. The novels provided an outlet for the necessary fantasy that a social outsider could fulfil his aspirations. More than that, by giving him an opportunity to shape events according to the directives of his imagination, they taught him that he could shape recalcitrant events in the world in which he lived. Furthermore, learning to push aside unpleasant thoughts and substitute an imaginative pattern of events later served him in good stead in his political career. Thus his resilience and imperturbability owed something to his ability to create and escape into imagined worlds.

Vivian Grey is one of the earliest examples of a novel in which a person's fundamental character is changed by experience. The more usual stress in prior English fiction was upon experience bringing out latent qualities that had been temporarily in eclipse. Such is the case in *Emma* and *Tom Jones*. When Vivian is toasted at Prince Lilliput's table, his mind reverts to an earlier occasion when Lord Courtown had toasted him at the Carabas home, ironically named Château Desir: 'Could he really be the same individual as the daring youth who then organized the crazy councils of those ambitious, imbecile greybeards? . . . He turned from the comparison with feelings of sickening disgust . . .' (VI, iii, p. 307). In the four books of the sequel, Vivian replaces Mr Grey as the mature resigned elder, and various figures take his place as the aspiring rogue.

Disraeli's fiction is never inhibited by those aesthetic conventions that stipulate that differing kinds of mimesis cannot co-exist in the same work. The reader's aesthetic pleasure derives in part from the dextrous movement from one kind of narrative to another, and the arousing of expectations that are not fulfilled in the expected way. *Vivian Grey* does not always benefit from its hodge-podge of genres, but in it Disraeli shows how the picaro tale and romance form need not be incompatible with scenes of psychological realism. An example is the scene in which Mrs Felix Lorraine tries to poison Vivian. Gothic melodrama presents the occasion for exploring psychological complexity in a way that recalls Jacobean tragedy. Disraeli may have lacked the vocabulary of modern psychology, but he knew how obsessions, fixations and darker impulses determine human behaviour. In this important regard, Disraeli parted company with the novels of manners and morals that Austen and Fielding had written and put himself in the tradition of Richardson, Emily Brontë and Hardy.

The psychologically subtle scene in which Disraeli uses Mrs Felix Lorraine as a dark parody of his own soul is one of the earliest appearances of the double motif in English fiction, outside the pure Gothic romance. When Mrs Felix Lorraine tries to poison Vivian, Disraeli effectively reveals Vivian's psychic complexity:

> I fancy that in this mysterious foreigner, that in this woman, I have met a kind of double of myself. The same wonderful knowledge of the human mind, the same sweetness of voice, the same miraculous management which had brought us both under the same roof; yet do I find her the most abandoned of all beings; a creature guilty of that which, even in the guilty age, I thought was obsolete and is it possible I am like her? . . . Am I all this time deceiving myself with some wretched sophistry? Am I, then, an intellectual Don Juan, reckless of human minds, as he was of human bodies; a spiritual libertine? (III, v, pp. 105–6)

Frightened by his own emotional and moral awareness, Vivian needs to reaffirm his Machiavellian self if only to preserve his own identity: 'Away with all fear, all repentance, all thought of past, all reckoning of future. If I be the Juan that I fancied myself, then Heaven be praised!' (III, v, p. 106).

Despite his flamboyant personality (embodied within the text in the narrative voice), Disraeli is quite a conventional moralist in *Vivian Grey*, particularly for one who speaks in the guise of a Byronic iconoclast. Even in this early novel the voice of the unconventional dandy and the passionate romantic is restrained by Disraeli's sense of propriety and a respect for moderation in passions. The early novels show hints of the self-control, intellectual discipline, pragmatism and deference to historical traditions that characterised Disraeli's behaviour in political circles. In *Vivian Grey*, he regards excessive ambition and unnatural lusts as diseases. Thus Mrs Lorraine's bursting a blood vessel in her final interview with Vivian is, within the novel's imagined world, a natural result of obsessive, self-indulgent behaviour. After the demise of Vivian's political plans, Disraeli makes clear the connection between his subsequent illness and Vivian's past moral behaviour: 'And what had been the past? It did indeed seem like a hot and feverish dream. Here was he once more in his own quiet room, watched over by his beloved parents' (IV, vi, p. 160). The one place of comfort where he is never under stress and where his ambition is constrained is in his parents' house.

Vivian's quest for a father figure may be related to Disraeli's own ambivalence towards a father who, as B. R. Jerman writes in *The Young Disraeli* 'had chosen a sedentary life for the same reason that he admonished his son for getting involved with the practical world: because practical affairs spelled struggle, misery, and almost certain defeat'.[6] At times the father anticipates Disraeli's wisdom figures, who will guide the protagonists in later novels; 'true happiness', according to Mr Grey, 'exists independent of the opinions or the intrigues of individuals: nor do I mean that glittering show of perpetual converse with the world which some miserable wanderers call Happiness; but that which can only be drawn from the sacred and solitary fountain of your own feelings' (III, ix, p. 132). But Mr Grey, like Disraeli's father on whom he is in part modelled, lives precisely by the 'perpetual converse' that he denounces.

Disraeli's attitude towards Vivian's father is as complex as his attitude towards his own father. Lucien Wolf may oversimplify the role of Vivian's father when he describes the first four books as 'a struggle between two standards of conduct – the selfish ambition, the unscrupulousness and cynicism of Vivian Grey, and the altruism, the self-respect, and optimism of his father'.[7] To be sure, when Vivian is immersed in his study of Platonists, his father counsels, 'Whether we are in this world in a state of probation for another, or whether we cease altogether when we cease to breathe, human feelings tell me that we have some duties to perform; to our fellow creatures, to our friends, to ourselves' (I, vi, 15–16). At first, Mr Grey seems the embodiment of a more mature conscience, invented by Disraeli to censor the behaviour of the self who, he grieved, had disappointed his father when his early expectations were unfulfilled. At a time when Disraeli himself contemplated retirement from the active life, he created a fictional counterpart – fathered a father – who himself had achieved happiness as part of a respectable social milieu and who had maintained his private existence.

Given Mr Grey's dilettantism, one wonders whether Disraeli meant us to view his father as the proper paradigm for Vivian to follow. While Disraeli relied upon Isaac D'Israeli when difficulties arose and praised his father generously in print, his independent spirit insisted that he separate himself from his father and view him critically. Fiction provided a sanctioned outlet for these attitudes. Mr Grey initiates Vivian into the 'moral hothouse' of London society. Nor should we forget the narrator's introduction of Mr Grey: 'He was a man of lettered tastes, and had hailed with no slight pleasure his succession to a fortune which, though limited in its duration, was still a great thing for a young lounger about town, not only with no profession, but with a mind unfitted for every species of business' (I, i, p. 2). It may be that Vivian's father imports worldliness and affectation into his life and is thus responsible in part for his moral myopia. The smug wisdom Mr Grey professes at the climax of the epistolary chapter is not without its ironic dimension when we recall that Mr Grey himself does not practise a life of altruism but rather indulges his own whims. Is his concept of 'social affections' on which 'true Fame, and true Happiness' rest different from his life as 'A Man of Chambers'? (I, i, p. 2; III, viii, p. 132). While Mr Grey speaks of high principles we cannot forget the life he has chosen. Yet Vivian's subsequent experience confirms the truth of many of his father's shibboleths. Although those truths are hardly equivalent to a value system or 'standard of conduct', they approximate the values held by the narrative voice and dramatised by the plot:

> Man is neither the vile nor the excellent being, which he sometimes imagines himself to be. He does not so much act by system, as by sympathy. . . . Let me warn you not to fall into the usual error of youth in fancying that the circle you move in is precisely the world itself. Do not imagine that there are not other beings, whose benevolent principle is governed by finer sympathies, by more generous passions, and by those nobler emotions which really constitute all our public and private virtues. (III, viii, p. 132)

Two versions of *Vivian Grey* survive, the more commonly read 1853 edition and the original 1826–7 edition. While the original reflects the man depicted in the first portrait, the later reflects the cautious political leader who very much wished to impress the English with his judgment and tact. To appreciate Disraeli's originality and precocity in his first novels, we should examine the text written in his early twenties. But to see how the mature Disraeli applied his *real* ambition to his own art, we need also to read the expurgated version. By juxtaposing the two editions, we get some understanding of how Disraeli changed as well as how he undermined his own art for the sake of his career.

The usual reasons given for Disraeli's expurgations is that in his later years Disraeli regarded *Vivian Grey* as an embarrassment, undoubtedly in part because its protagonist, whose early history recognisably paralleled his own, is unscrupulous and conniving in his pursuit of power. It might be more accurate to say that Disraeli felt that he should publicly regard the novel as an awkward vestige of his youth because it rekindled memories, in the minds of enemies and supporters, of his extravagant youthful behaviour. The introduction to the 1853 edition is an apology for reprinting the novel at all, and exhibits unaccustomed humility: 'Books written by boys . . . which pretend to give a picture of manners, and to deal in knowledge of human nature, must necessarily be founded on affectation'. As Robert Blake notices, and as comparison of the early edition confirms, the 1853 edition plays down Vivian's impudence and unscrupulousness as well as the narrator's irreverent and playful attitude towards his early machinations.[8] As a political figure, it behoved Disraeli to omit passages that might have helped win the reader's sympathy for Vivian, sympathy that reflected Disraeli's original ambivalence towards his young picaro. Thus the following passage is expurgated in 1853:

> But doubting of all things, he doubted of himself; and finding himself so changed from what he had been only a year or two before, he felt as if he should not be astonished if he changed again. . . .
>
> With all his grief, he was no cynic – if he smiled on men it was not in bitterness; if he thought them base, he did not blame them. He pitied those whose baseness, in his opinion, was their sufficient punishment. . . . Subdued, but not melancholy; contemplative, but not gloomy; he left his solitude. (V. 1)

Much of the behaviour that follows dramatises and validates this description.

In the 1826 edition, Disraeli's sympathies are with his alter ego Vivian, even when the latter is morally obtuse or has disgraced himself. In 1853 he omits the crucial last sentence of Book IV: 'I fear me much, that Vivian Grey is a lost man; but, I am sure that every sweet and gentle spirit, who has read the sad story of his fortunes, will breathe a holy prayer this night, for his restoration to society, and to himself' (IV, vi). Nor does he include the defensive response with which he began the sequel, a response which reflects his dismay at being condemned for the failings of his fictional character, and which in turn blames the *Zeitgeist* for Vivian's flaws:

> I conceived the character of a youth of great talents, whose mind had been corrupted, as the minds of many of our youth have been, by the artificial age in which he lived. The age was not less corrupted than the being it had generated. In his whole career he was to be pitied; but for his whole career he was to be punished. . . . I am blamed for the affectation, the flippancy, the arrogance, the wickedness of his fictitious character. Yet was Vivian Grey to talk like Simon Pure, and act like Sir Charles Grandison? (V. i)

But neither edition quite sustains Jerman's contention that *Vivian Grey* is a plea for the protagonist: 'Disraeli's purpose . . . was to open the hearts of society to misbegotten lads like Vivian, not to harden him. Society, he guessed, would agree with him, pat him on the back, and not only restore Vivian to fame and fortune, but also acclaim him, Ben, the new Byron'.[9]

To be sure, one doubts whether Disraeli, who conceived himself as Byron's heir, was really distraught at being identified with Vivian. It is probable that in 1826 he would have enjoyed the attention. But in his view the original and the sequel showed that Vivian Grey was punished for his vices. Certainly the last four books emphasise the sincerity and seriousness of Vivian's feelings after he is purged of his bogeyman, ambition. In the 1853 edition, Disraeli sought to emphasise his condemnation of Vivian by stressing the ironic distance between the narrator and Vivian.

Part of Disraeli's embarrassment with Vivian Grey derives from Vivian's abuse of political power and his subsequent disgust with public life. After all, the fictive character turned his back on the life to which Disraeli had devoted himself. Furthermore, in 1853 the mature Disraeli, the leader of his party, would not have accepted the chastened Vivian's fatalism; nor would he have wanted readers to be reminded that a character with whom he had been identified in the public's mind had lapsed into melancholy and passivity. When the woman he loves reveals herself as the Archduchess, Vivian passively accepts the demise of his hopes: 'He looked up to Heaven with a wild smile, half of despair and half of defiance. It seemed to imply that Fate had now done her worst, and that he had at last the satisfaction of knowing himself to be the most unfortunate and unhappy being that ever existed' (VIII, i, pp. 463). Vivian's misfortune in love – one woman has been denied to him by reason of death (Violet Fane) and one has been denied to him because of aristocratic ties (the Baroness) – reflected Disraeli's spasms of self-pity in 1826–7.

Disraeli deleted from the 1853 edition the very effective portrait of Dr Von Spittergen, a physician who lives a pastoral life with his loyal, capable daughter. The doctor and his daughter have an important thematic function because they are antithetical to the host of characters who have polished manners and hollow principles. Although they are presented as virtual cartoons – he insults his patients and she is a six-foot Amazon – they represent Disraeli's naive ideal of the truly moral people. From them Vivian learns how inferior an acquaintance with the world is to a knowledge of Nature. The daughter provokes his most penetrating soliloquy. She has just told him that she had dreamed of being a heroine in a romance and 'lived in a world of my own creation . . . [where] I formed no conception of the existence of duties' (VII, vi). But her father's misery after he lost both his wife and his son awakened her to a sense of duty. Vivian understands the parallel:

> His early, his insane career, flitted across his mind. He would have stifled the remembrance with a sigh; but man is the slave of Memory. He, too, had thought himself a peculiar creature; he, too, had lived in a world of his own creation; he, too, had sacrificed himself to an idea: he, too, had looked upon his fellow-creatures as the puppets of his will. Would that his reveries had been as harmless as this maiden's! Would that he could compensate for his errors, and forget his follies in a life of activity, of usefulness, of beneficence! To the calm satisfaction and equal tenor of such a life, why had he madly preferred the wearing anxiety, the consuming care, the eternal vigilance, the constant contrivance, the agonising suspense, the distracting vicissitudes of his own career? Alas! it is our nature to sicken, from our birth, after some object of unattainable felicity – to struggle through the freshest years of our life in an insane pursuit after some indefinite good, which does not even exist! (VII, vi)

When Disraeli moved this *contemptus mundi* passage to Beckendorff's house in the 1853 edition, he made some important changes. He deleted the words 'his insane' and shortened the passage between 'memory' and 'wearing anxiety' to read: 'For a moment he mused over Power; but then he, shuddering, shrank from the wearing anxiety, the consuming care, the eternal vigilance, the constant contrivance, the agonising suspense, the distracting vicissitudes of his past career' (VI, vii, pp. 356–7). Because, despite his protests, readers had insisted on identifying him with Vivian, Disraeli did not want to put the passage about 'usefulness' and 'beneficence' in the optative case; presumably he had fulfilled those hopes by 1853. Both recognition of duty and concern for others are central principles of the Young England novels, but the pastoralism of the doctor and his daughter, attractive as it may have seemed to Disraeli in the late 1820s, is a value that in 1853 Disraeli, the party leader and former Chancellor of the Exchequer had firmly rejected.

Disraeli was very conscious of, if somewhat patronising about, literary traditions and genres in 1826, even if he later denied reading novels other than those he wrote. While *Vivian Grey*, is often thought of as a Silver Fork novel in the tradition of Plumer Ward's *Tremaine* (1825), and Bulwer Lytton's *Pelham* (1828), it is more accurate to say that it is a parody of that kind of novel. *Vivian Grey* is a direct heir of *Tristram Shandy* and *Don Juan* in its playful self-consciousness. It is a parody both of the *Bildungsroman* and of novel writing itself. Disraeli's style and tone are as much the subject as the history of Vivian Grey. As Vivian carries Mrs Felix Lorraine to her bedchambers after she has fainted, the narrator opens the next chapter by ostentatiously stepping back from the couple in the bedroom:

> What is this chapter to be about? Come, I am inclined to be courteous! You shall choose the subject of it. What shall it be, sentiment or scandal? a love-scene or a lay-sermon? You shall not choose? Then we must open the note which Vivian, in the morning, found on his pillow. . . . In some future book, probably the twentieth or twenty-fifth, when the plot begins to wear threadbare, and we can afford a digression, I may give a chapter on Domestic Tactics. (III, vii, pp. 116–17)

Such passages deliberately dispel the illusion that the narrator is someone who exists within the narrative world and call attention to the conventions on which fiction depends. Moreover, Disraeli is good-naturedly chiding the reader for participating in a farcical relationship in which his whims determine what the reader will know. In the 1853 editions of both *Vivian Grey* and *The Young Duke*, Disraeli dilutes the role of the self-dramatising narrator as a figure who calls attention to the fact that he is creating an artifice which requires the reader's participation. The exuberant self-mockery of the above passage goes much further in the original text:

> What is this chapter to be about? Come, I'm inclined to be courteous! You shall choose the subject of it. What shall it be – sentiment or scandal? a love scene, or a lay-sermon – or a lecture on omelette soufflées? I am sick of the world! . . . and actually am now hesitating whether I shall turn misanthrope, or go to the Ancient Music. Not that you are to imagine that I am a dissatisfied, disappointed, moody monster, who lectures the stars, and fancies himself Rousseau secundus – not in the least. (III, vii)

As the above quotation makes clear, the boisterous, extravagant prose of the original places Vivian's fall in a comic context that prevents our taking it too seriously. The ironic relationship between style and substance, between voice and plot, makes the reader question whether moral certainty is possible or desirable and prevents him from feeling confident about his own judgments. Part of the *aesthetic* pleasure in reading *Vivian Grey* is our own inability to gain a moral foothold, our continuing quest for positional assurance. Even in the less lively 1853 edition, Disraeli's scintillating wit, ironic observations, feisty tone, and exuberant prose style enliven every page and make reading Disraeli a distinct delight, although at times his plot and theme meander. In a sense, the original epigraph to *Vivian Grey* ('Why then the world's mine oyster, /which I with sword will open') applies not only to the early attitude of Vivian, but to the ebullient persona which dominates the 1826–7 novel; his ebullience is barely contained except when the protagonist suffers reversal and disappointment.[10]

Disraeli is indebted to Byron's *Don Juan* for his eccentric, arrogant and delightful narrator. The high-spirited chapter ii of Book IV of the original is, except for the first sentence, entirely left out of the 1853 edition. The omitted chapter, ironically entitled 'Development of the Plot' (chapter titles were omitted in the 1853 edition), is a soliloquy in which the narrator displays his impudence, wit, and volubility. In this chapter he chases an insect, lies down in response to the luncheon bell, and remains at rest until he hears the dinner bell. He finally claims to be bored by a lavish dinner although he eats every course. While Disraeli's apparent point is to call attention to the difficulty of writing, the *effect* is to prevent the reader from having the illusion of being transported into Vivian Grey's world. The reader is simultaneously conscious of the nominal subject, Vivian Grey; of the speaker's own idiosyncratic vision as he engaged in the act of telling; and of his own world outside art of which he is continually made aware by the speaker's dispelling the illusion that he or the speaker is actually contained within Vivian's world:

> I had intended to have commenced this book with something quite terrific – a murder or a marriage: and I find that all my great ideas have ended in a lounge . . . I have not felt so well for these six months. . . . Now I don't know what I shall do. I think I'll amuse myself by jumping over that *ha-ha*. . . . Good Heavens! I'm afraid I'm getting healthy!
>
> Now for Vivian Grey again! I don't know how it is, but I cannot write today, the room's so hot. – Open that door – now I shall get on better. Oh, what a wretched pen! I can't get out a sentence. The room's too cold; – shut the horrid door. Write I must, and will, – what's the matter? It's this great bowstring of a cravat. Off with it! who could ever write in cravat? (IV, ii)

Disraeli's ventriloquism enables him to mimic Sterne's idiosyncratic style – a style which depends upon short, darting phrases to mime the erratic movement of human thought. While Joyce and Proust have taken stream of consciousness infinitely further, in 1826 Disraeli's technique was daring and innovative, particularly for a novel that was more melodrama and romance than an exploration of the speaker's psyche. No writer except for Sterne either approached the degree to which Disraeli's omniscient narrator becomes an audacious presence within the text or more subtly attempted to involve the audience in the consciousness of a self-dramatising character. The voice *creates himself* in the same way as Vivian does in the English chapters, and as Beckendorff and Esper George do on the continent. Although Disraeli failed in his first attempt to play a potentially significant public role when he helped to launch the abortive newspaper entitled *The Representative*, he learned how imagination and ambition could create the self a person wished to be. Creating characters, Disraeli discovered, is the business not only of the author, but of any man who seeks wealth and power to which he is not born.

III

Disraeli probably wrote *The Young Duke* during the winter of 1829–30 when he had lost money in the stock market and may even have landed in debtors' prison. In any case, he surely needed money for his trip to the Middle East, a trip which he undoubtedly hoped would be the inspiration to help him finish *Alroy*. Disraeli felt that in succumbing to the temptation of Colburn, the publisher of *Vivian Grey* who paid him the rather handsome fee of £500 for *The Young Duke*, he was prostituting his talents.[11] It must have seemed to Disraeli's hyperbolic sensibility that the very writing of the novel, when he should have been writing serious works such as *Alroy* or *Popanilla* (1828), was a waste of his talents comparable to his title character's prodigality.

The Young Duke, like *Vivian Grey*, is a tale of moral degeneration followed by moral redemption. *The Young Duke's* subject is the dissipation and eventual enlightenment of George Augustus Frederick, Duke of St. James, who upon reaching his twenty-first birthday becomes one of the wealthiest men in Europe. His father, the late Duke, had appointed Mr Dacre as guardian to his orphan son; Dacre is a responsible, upright gentleman of an old Catholic family. But his son's upbringing had fallen into the hands of his brother-in-law, Lord Fitz-Pompey, when Dacre had to leave England because of his wife's illness. The lesson that the impressionable adolescent learns from Fitz-Pompey is that the latter's 'exertions . . . have saved him from a life of stern privation and irrational restraint' (I, ii, p. 5). The Duke is morally unequipped for the fashionable world into which he is catapulted, or for the wealth that he suddenly has at his disposal. At first, he is a spoiled adolescent, 'a sublime coxcomb . . . whose finished manner and shrewd sense combined to prevent [his] conceit from being contemptible' (I, iv, p. 13). But he begins to succumb to solipsism when he is affected by the adulation he receives: 'He could no longer resist the conviction that he was a superior essence. . . . The world seemed created solely for his enjoyment' (I, x, p. 34). He renews his friendship with Dacre's daughter, who is more polished and accomplished than those jaded aristocrats in the Fitz-Pompey circle. Subsequently the generous affection, natural grace, and manners of the Dacres, particularly of the daughter, have a significant influence on his ethical development. While the Dacres are responsible aristocrats, interested in those who live within the environs of their estates, Sir Lucious Grafton is the antitype who is concerned only with personal gratification. (Appropriately his first name suggests 'luscious', and his second suggests both 'graft' and a foreshortened version of 'gratification'.) He will even secretly encourage his wife's adultery so that he might obtain a divorce. Disraeli satirises an aristocracy whose lives revolve around banquets and parties and lack sustaining moral values.

The novel's basic structural principle is that the Duke gradually chooses the example of the upstanding Dacres, the Catholics who 'lived as proscribed in the realm which they had created', and rejects the amoral aristocrats, epitomised by Sir Lucious and Mrs Dallington Vere, a twenty-three-year-old widow who lacks standards or scruples (II, iv, p. 63). When the young Duke receives Fitz-Pompey's final letter and learns of Mrs Dallington Vere's machinations, he undergoes the final step of moral conversion; he 'turned with trembling and disgust from these dark terminations of unprincipled careers; and these fatal evidences of the indulgence of unbridled passions. How nearly, too, had he been shipwrecked in this moral whirlpool! With what gratitude did he not invoke the beneficent Providence that had not permitted the innate seeds of human virtue to be blighted in his wild and neglected soul!' (V, xiii, p. 324). This passage not only brings to a climax the Duke's characterisation and gives shape and structure to much, if not all, of the narrative; it also shows how Disraeli can render a self-recognition scene efficiently and movingly when his plot requires it.

As the novel progresses, Disraeli, through his surrogate, the narrator, becomes surprisingly sympathetic to the young Duke, considering the latter's early moral lapses and his seeming superficiality. As soon as the young Duke is captivated by May Dacre and begins to emerge from his self-enchantment, the narrator drops his detachment which in the early chapters seemed to border on cool disdain. May awakens latent impulses that enable the Duke to transcend his self-love: 'The Duke of St. James was in one of his sublime fits. He had commenced by thinking of May Dacre, and he ended by thinking of himself. He was under that delicious and dreamy excitement which we experience when the image of a lovely and beloved object begins to mix itself up without intense self-love' (II, x, p. 96). After the Duke is rebuked by May, the narrator perceives the Duke no longer as a remote aristocrat, but as a person whose emotions are of interest to him. When the narrator speaks of the experience of waking from 'our' first delusion, he drops his ironic stance and reveals his kinship with the disillusionment of the Duke:

'For then we first feel the nothingness of self; the hell of sanguine spirits. All is dreary, blank and cold' (II, xiv, p. 118). Book II ends with the Duke disappointed in love, but established in our sympathies: 'There seemed not on the earth's face a more forlorn, a more feeble, a less estimable wretch than himself' (II, xiv, p. 118). The riches and conspicuous waste in which the narrator has immersed the Duke (and which Disraeli enjoyed describing) seem painfully irrelevant. The speaker's condescending tone to the young, irresponsible aristocrat ('But it is a great thing to be a young Duke') is no longer quite appropriate now that his emotional life is revealed as both intense and complicated (II, xiii, p. 109).

When Disraeli wished, he could be as graphic and precise a realist as any nineteenth-century novelist, but as an artist Disraeli did not feel it either necessary or desirable to adhere to realism. While the generic mix is not always an asset, various kinds of mimesis coexist in his novels. In *The Young Duke*, to our regret, he includes formulated and clichéd descriptions of country estates which owe something to British landscape painting in the eighteenth century; melodrama in its worst Gothic excesses; and cartoon figures who might better have been more developed characters. Yet he can deftly select a specific incident to mime the world in which he lived and to typify a social and moral milieu. An example is the scene in which the Duke succumbs to the temptation of gambling, perhaps the most effective scene in the first two full-length novels. Within the company of the dissipated group, our sympathies for the Duke increase because he is gulled by men beside whom he is a mere novice. Disraeli depicts excessive gambling as a kind of moral cannibalism, whose obsessed practitioners abandon civility and lose their fundamental sanity:

> No attempt at breakfast now, no affectation of making a toilet or airing the room. The atmosphere was hot, to be sure, but it well became such a Hell. There they sat, in total, in positive forgetfulness of everything but the hot game they were hunting down. There was not a man in the room except Tom Cogit, who could have told you the name of the town in which they were living. There they sat, almost breathless, watching every turn with the fell look in their cannibal eyes which showed their total inability to sympathise with their fellow-beings. All forms of society had long been forgotten. There was no snuff-box handed about now, for courtesy, admiration, or a pinch; no affectation of occasionally

making a remark upon any other topic but the all-engrossing one. (IV, viii, p. 244–5)

Disraeli's prose subtly implies that such compulsive behaviour deprives civilisation of its underpinnings: courtesy, civility and balance. He does this by rendering the claustrophobic ambience of the room and the participants' loss of their social selves. That the Duke is more appalled by the effects of gambling upon his soul than upon his purse separates him from his fellows. Yet the Duke recognises his kinship with those he despises. With horror, he sees how his worst impulses have gained sway over what he considers his real self. Looking into an actual and internal mirror, he sees that he has involuntarily created a mask for his true self: 'As he looked upon his fellow gamesters, he seemed, for the first time in his life, to gaze upon some of these hideous demons of whom he had read. He looked in the mirror at himself. A blight seemed to have fallen over his beauty, and his presence seemed accursed' (IV, viii, p. 245). The gamblers are, in one sense, an external correlative to the dissipation and self-indulgence that have characterised the Duke's life since his twenty-first birthday. The ghouls that have to be purged are not so much the present company but the values that have gradually taken hold.

If it was not until *Sybil* (1845) that Disraeli learned to structure his chapters consistently and to arrange them so as to present a dramatised argument, it was in part because in his early work he conceived himself as a performer and comedian as much as a satirist and polemicist. Yet *The Young Duke*, despite occasional lapses, shows that Disraeli's sense of narrative unity had evolved since *Vivian Grey*. While the novel has a variety of character sketches, narrative digressions and social satire befitting Disraeli's characteristic merging of genres – here most notably romance, burlesque and realistic novel – it is held together by a tighter conception of plot structure than *Vivian Grey* or *Popanilla*. The closing movement, beginning with the Duke's awakening to the horror of his dissipated life, has a taut morality structure which, as it reorders the significance of prior episodes, casts a pall over the 'silver fork' glitter of the novel. For example, the scene in which the Duke journeys to London to make his political debut illustrates the development of Disraeli's artistry, to a point where many of the digressive episodes bear at least some organic relationship to the novel's major action and central themes. Like Fielding's Man of the Hill section in *Tom Jones*, the scene in the coach provides a moral context for the action. The Duke meets a sailor who praises marriage and who comically foreshadows the Duke's blissful marriage to May Dacre. The vanity of the pompous philosopher, Duncan Macmorrough, Senior, contrasts with the Duke's new humility, while his bombast contrasts with the Duke's restrained dignity. The example of young Duncan as an influential leader of the utilitarians gives the young Duke additional incentive. Disraeli undoubtedly uses the Macmorroghs to satirise the Mills. Not only did Disraeli dislike utilitarianism, but his pride and ambition may have caused him to regard John Stuart Mill's precocious genius and prominence with envy.[12] Within the coach he learns of the dissipation of a young man named Charles Burnet, who has frittered away his money in dalliances with women. That Burnet reminds the Duke of his own errors and gives him a chance to respond generously is further indication of his moral growth: 'If I had been in this youth's station, my career probably would have been as fatal. Let me assist her. Alas! how I have misused my power, when even to do this slight deed, I am obliged to hesitate, and consider whether it be practicable' (V, vii, p. 299).

Although Disraeli conceived *The Young Duke* as a commercial venture, it was also the first of many occasions when he dramatised the intellectual and moral life of an aristocrat. In Disraeli's aristocratic novels, his protagonists are often a kind of moral elect whose inherent quality enables them to transcend their own boredom or dissipation or both. This category includes Contarini, Ferdinand Armine (*Henrietta Temple*), Cadurcis (*Venetia*), Lothair, Endymion, and the heroes of all three Young England novels. As is true of *Coningsby*, *Henrietta Temple* and *Lothair*, other *Bildungsromane* in the Disraeli canon, *The Young Duke* is structured as a morality play with various tempters struggling for the soul and intellect of an aristocratic protagonist. (This is even more true of the 1853 edition where the ebullient narrator plays a less prominent role.)

While much of the novel until the climactic gambling scene reveals Disraeli's fascination with the dissipated circle in which the young Duke lives, and with the worldly pleasures of the wealthy, the Duke's conversion gives the novel a stronger moral dimension than most readers have allowed it. Again we see Disraeli, the dandy and self-styled heir to Byron, imposing traditional standards upon his hero. In *The Young Duke*, Disraeli dramatises a rebellious temperament only to show that such a temperament must adjust to community standards and renounce some of its individuality. In temperament as well as in politics, the man who first ran as a Radical before converting to Toryism was even in the early 1830s far more conservative than he thought himself.

While Disraeli did not regard *The Young Duke* as part of 'the secret history of his feelings', it is difficult to separate Disraeli from the young Duke's conflict between self-indulgence and responsibility. Disraeli's surrogate, the narrative voice, vacillates revealingly from a worldly jaded tone to a self-consciousness about his own situation. Lucien Wolf claims that Disraeli had experienced and enjoyed the extravagant world in which the Duke lives.[13] Thus it may have been crucial to Disraeli's own self-image to show that the Duke's inherent quality protected him from permanent corruption. In any case, the Duke's real self seems immune to the effects of drinking, gambling and adultery. The narrator's self-denigration may be related to Disraeli's disgust with the vapid social world in which he has been living, a world which Disraeli's narrator implies that he, to his regret, belongs: 'The manoeuvres and tactics of society are infinitely more numerous and infinitely finer than those of strategy. . . . And this glare, and heat, and noise, this congeries of individuals without sympathy and dishes without flavour; this is society! What an effect without a cause!' (III, vii, pp. 151–53).

Disraeli's social satire of the aristocracy and of England's profligacy may have reflected his own resentment in the late 1820s and early 1830s of a society, and particularly a ruling class, that had not recognised his merit. Some of the narrator's bitterness may also be the result of his own frustrated quest for power and prominence: 'Born in the most artificial country of this most artificial age, was it wonderful that I imbibed its false views, and shared its fatal passions?' (IV, xviii). But this scathing remark was bowdlerised from the 1853 edition. Omitting the passages that give the speaker an interest of his own changes the novel significantly. The original novel's interest depended upon the double vision of the tale and teller. In the first edition, the speaker's consciousness of his own shortcomings and his own vacillation between high-spirited worldiness and malaise make him a kind of double of the protagonist. Disraeli's chameleonic speaker is alternately performer, virtuoso and Byronic hero; we attend to his presence and ventriloquism as surely as we do to Thackeray's puppeteer. By calling attention to the artifice that he is creating, Disraeli emphasises how the people he is describing have created artifices in their lives, and have reduced themselves to one-dimensional characters in a comedy of manners.

In *The Young Duke*, we see the first seeds of the concept – so prominent in The Young England novels – that England must have a politically conscientious aristocracy. The young Duke's progress into a responsible member of *res publica* illustrates a cornerstone of Disraeli's political philosophy. For he believed that a self-indulgent aristocracy had abnegated its responsibilities as moral leaders of the nation.[14] That the Duke gives his first speech on the subject of Catholic Emancipation demonstrates Disraeli's commitment to this cause, and the cause it represented for him—the opening of the political processes to outsiders and minorities, including Jews. Throughout his career he supported extending the suffrage; he maintained, 'the wider the popular suffrage the more powerful would be the natural aristocracy' – by which he meant the aristocracy of ability.[15] Although as a convert, he was not pursuing his self-interest, he understood that any intrinsic barriers would have affected his chances for election to Parliament and higher office. The Duke overcomes despair, revives his own soul by discovering another to complete himself, and commits himself to political life; thus he fulfils Disraeli's public and private fantasies.

Disraeli uses *The Young Duke* to propose tentatively one of his later political ideas. This occurs when the memory of May Dacre interrupts the Duke in his imaginative meditation upon his moral decline:

> He felt a criminal. In the darkness of his meditation a flash burst from his lurid mind, a celestial light appeared to dissipate this thickening gloom, and his soul felt as if it were bathed with the softening radiancy. He thought of May Dacre, he thought of everything that was pure, and holy, and beautiful, and luminous, and calm. It was the innate virtue of the man that made this appeal to his corrupted nature. (IV, viii, p. 246)

The Duke responds to May as if she were a saint; he recalls her in terms that would be applicable to the Virgin Mary. This pattern of a Protestant hero's captivation by the innocent purity of a Catholic young woman is repeated in *Sybil*. It constitutes Disraeli's naïve allegory about the necessity of merging Protestantism with its pure antecedent, Catholicism. (Although Disraeli was a converted Anglican, at the age of twenty-five he did not take very seriously theological divisions between Anglicanism and Catholicism and probably regarded such divisions as silly family quarrels.) When Disraeli, albeit naïvely, suggests a procedure for national religious reconciliation, he anticipates one of his major political principles –

the need for national unity at a time when England was torn by class, religious and political strife. His concept of Tory democracy and his own role as national leader derived from his view that the Whigs represented the aristocracy, while the Tories represented the monarchy and the people. During the difficult passage of the Second Reform Bill, he said 'I feel great hope of . . . realizing the dream of my life, and re-establishing Toryism on a national foundation'.[16] To Disraeli, a converted Anglican who thought in nationalistic terms, theological differences were most significant in terms of their political effects. After the aggressive papal initiative of 1850, Disraeli's sympathies for Catholics ebbed as we shall discover in *Lothair* (1870).[17]

We may compare the original 1831 edition with the 1853 edition to see how Disraeli the artist recreated his past to present a respectable image of a party leader who aspired to be Prime Minister. Orginally, the speaker is an exuberant, multifaceted ironist in the tradition of Sterne and Disraeli's own *Vivian Grey*. However, the Disraeli of 1853 wished to assume a stance of maturity and detachment and was no doubt embarrassed by the speaker's erratic, if moving, solipsism. Although critics have regarded *The Young Duke* as the one objective work among Disraeli's early novels, nevertheless he has dramatised the full range of his doubts, anxieties and aspirations. The bowdlerised 1853 edition plays down his self-pity, arrogance and rodomontade. Behind his 1831 pose lies a note of desperation: 'What I am, I know not, nor do I care. I have that within me, which man can neither give nor take away, which can throw light on the darkest passages of life, and draw, from a discordant world, a melody divine' (III, xviii). Such personal outbursts overwhelm the narrative voice and reveal Disraeli's cry of despair in a world that has not accepted him at his own valuation. Given his feeling that he had interrupted his serious work on *Alroy* to write *The Young Duke* for commercial reasons, he may have been asserting his aesthetic and moral purity. Like the Duke, he believes that he is protected by his intrinsic quality. The original edition places greater stress on the speaker's feeling that he has betrayed his better self. Perhaps wishing for an enduring heterosexual relationship, he thinks of his soul in terms that parallel those with which the Duke thinks of his beloved May Dacre. Speaking directly to his soul, he repents for his past conduct: 'I feel that I have betrayed thee. Hadst thou been the inmate of more spiritual clay, bound with a brain less headstrong, and with blood less hot, thou mightest have been glorious.' He addresses his soul as if it were a woman whom he had betrayed: 'Oh! mistress that I have loved – Oh! idol that I have ever worshipped! how like a fond wife, who clings even closer when we wrong her most, how faithful art thou, even in this hour of need, and how consoling is thy whispering voice!' (III, xviii). It may be that as Disraeli is renouncing his own dissipation, he needs to purge his baser instincts and passions and rescue his better ones.

In 1853 the older Disraeli wished to suppress the more idiosyncratic aspects of his sometimes high-spirited, sometimes morbid, and sometimes manic speaker. For example, in the 1831 edition, when May refuses the Duke's offer of marriage and pointedly gives as her reason his inconstancy, the narrator interrupts his tale to comment:

> The scene should have been touching; but I know not why, when I read it over, it seems to me a tissue of half-meanings. What I meant is stamped upon my brain; but I have lost the power of conveying what I feel, if indeed that power were ever mine. I write with an aching head and quivering hand; yet I must write, if but to break the solitude, which is to me a world quick with exciting life; I scribble to divert a brain, which, though weak, will struggle with strong thoughts, and lest my mind should muse itself to madness.
>
> . . . Mind is a fine thing, I won't deny it, and mine was once as full of pride and hope as an infant empire. But where are now my deeds and aspirations, and where the fame I dreamed of when a boy? I find the world just slipping through my fingers, and cannot grasp the jewel ere it falls. I quit on earth, where none will ever miss me, save those whose blood requires no laurels to make them love my memory. My life has been a blunder and a blank, and all ends by my adding one more slight ghost to the shadowy realm of fatal precocity! These are the rubs that make us feel the vanity of life – the littleness of man. Yet I do not groan, and will not murmur. My punishment is no caprice of tyranny. I brought it on myself, as greater men have done before; but I think my case is most like Nebuchadnezzar's. (III, xviii)

His view of himself as Prometheus and Nebuchadnezzar and the image of his mind as an empire that is slipping away anticipate the hyperbolic fantasies of *Contarini Fleming* and especially *Alroy*. For no sooner do we take seriously a passage like the preceding one than the erratic speaker snaps out of his self-pity and gloom, and begins to reveal an independent self who has established his literary reputation despite the scorn of the critics and the artificiality of age. Finally, he affirms his commitment to England and his hope for a career of public service rather than literature, and he does so in terms that suggest he can ameliorate England's ills:

> Oh, England! – Oh! My country – not in hate I left thee – not in bitterness am I wandering here and my heart is thine, although my shadow falls upon a foreign strand; and although many an Eastern clime and Southern race have given something of their burning blood, it flows for thee. Farewell, my country! Few can love thee better than he who traces here these idle lines . . . if ever the hour shall call, my brain and life are thine. (III, xviii)

Beyond the hyperbole lies Disraeli's ambition to devote his life to England and his desire to merge his destiny with that of his country.

IV

As Jerman has remarked, *Contarini Fleming: A Psychological Romance* is Disraeli's *A Portrait of the Artist as a Young Man*. 'Disraeli's fictionalized autobiography . . . reflects his own reveries, doubts, miseries, failures and despair, dredged up out of the past and only slightly disguised.'[18] Disraeli's third novel, published in 1832 when he was still only twenty-seven, mimes his poetic and psychological development. In *Contarini*, external events are a correlative to Contarini's state of mind. Yet, Disraeli is most concerned with creating words and images that reflect his own inner feelings. To understand what he is trying to do, we might recall T. S. Eliot's definition of objective correlative: 'The only way of expressing emotion in the form of art is by finding an objective correlative; in other words, a set of objects, a situation, a chain of events which shall be the formula of that *particular* emotion; such that when the external facts, which must terminate in sensory experience, are given, the emotion is immediately evoked'.[19] Contarini may nominally have an independent existence but he is inseparable from Disraeli's own complex personality and character. Disraeli does not succeed in creating a sufficient distinction between himself and his character. While Contarini is meant to be Disraeli's version of the poetic personality, he is really a representation of Disraeli's own psyche. Disraeli the romantic uses Contarini to dramatise how his own imagination will free his soul from conventions, traditions, systems and false knowledge.

Like *Vivian Grey*, *Contarini Fleming: A Psychological Romance* is about its title character's ambitious quest for public recognition. But Contarini cannot make up his mind whether to devote his energies to literature or to politics. Nor could Disraeli. He wrote *Contarini* when he felt conflicting impulses. At the same time as he adopted the pose of a dandy heedless of the opinions and judgments of society, he wished to make a mark within the world whose values he flouted. Disraeli's dandyism is something other than the aberration it would have been in the later Victorian years. As Blake has written, the 1830s constituted 'a period of extravagance, affectation, frivolity, and artifice'.[20] Unconventional behaviour and the posture of rebellion against traditions and convention were more acceptable than in the later Victorian years, just as they were more acceptable in the United States in the late 1960s and early 1970s than in the 1950s. Disraeli was influenced by the unconventional social and moral behaviour of Count d'Orsay, to whom he dedicated *Henrietta Temple*, as well as by his close friend, Bulwer Lytton; the latter was a Member of Parliament, and a dandy who cut a flamboyant, eccentric figure while enjoying public attention and flouting middle-class standards. On the one hand Disraeli disregarded the manners and morals of the middle class and the staid aristocrats who dominated the Tories and viewed them from an iconoclastic perspective and, on the other, he wished to enter Parliament, albeit at first as a Radical; indeed, he lost his first race in the very year, 1832, in which *Contarini* was published. Disraeli's oscillation (as well as Contarini's) between poet and politician reflected the changing fortunes of his own career as well as his need to use his writing to pay his debts. It may be that the death of William Meredith, his close friend and the fiancé of his sister, while the two men were on their grand tour in 1830 also had something to do with the novel's ambivalence about worldly ambition. No sooner does Contarini achieve something, than he feels guilty and troubled, and denounces success in the world of action. It is as if Disraeli wrote the novel with an acute sense of the transience of worldly success.

In his 1845 preface Disraeli claims that he imagined another self, a double, whose psychological development mirrored his own:

> When the author meditated over the entireness of the subject, it appeared to him that the autobiographical form was a necessary condition of a successful fulfilment. . . . Having adopted this

conclusion, the author then endeavoured to conceive a character whose position in life should be at variance, and, as it were, in constant conflict with his temperament; and the accidents of whose birth, nevertheless, tended to develop his psychology. (p. vi)

What Disraeli has done is to create a mask whose superficial social circumstances and biography differ from his own, but whose subjective life mirrors his own life. Contarini is born with the advantages Disraeli lacked: nobility, wealth and a politically prominent family. While Disraeli is still an obscure figure, very much affected by his past setbacks, Contarini, at the novel's end, is building 'a scene which may rival in beauty and variety, although not in extent, the villa of Hadrian' (VII, ii, p. 372).

Because his mother was an Italian and his father a native of a different European country, Contarini feels that he is an outsider and a temperamental stranger in the unspecified northern country where his father holds office. Perhaps mirroring his own difficulties with his mother, Disraeli makes Contarini's mother unresponsive to Contarini's emotional and imaginative needs. Contarini vacillates between a desire to pursue his art and his urge to excel, as his father has, in the affairs of the world.

Visions, dreams and fictions occupy young Contarini's mind. In a passage that echoes the Preface to the *Lyrical Ballads*, Contarini says that he writes in search of 'relief from the overwhelming vitality of thought in the flowing spirit of poetic creation' (I, i, p. 4). Just as he now finds an outlet for his feelings in creative activity, throughout his life his imagination provides him with solace from stress and turmoil. Even as a child when he feels unloved by his stepmother, he imagines his aunt's garden as a 'fine world' where he 'wandered about in quest of some strange adventure' (I, iii, pp. 8–9). When as a youngster he encounters Christiana, his imagination transforms the adolescent girl into a private myth: she 'was the heroine of all my sports. Now I had indeed a princess' (I, iv, p. 12). Transforming her into a character within his own world is a prelude to his creating a fantasy love who will not have other commitments and interests. He names this woman 'Egeria', after the mythical advisor of Numa Pompilius; the psychological cause of this vision is his realisation that Christiana was kindly to other people, including a boy two years older than he. The woman of the vision 'was not unlike Christiana, but more dazzling and very pensive' (I, vi, p. 20). His obsession with Magdalen – perhaps indicative of Disraeli's fascination with Catholic rituals and ceremonies – is a successor to his pre-adolescent sexual fantasies, Christiana and Egeria. 'Each year my mistress seemed to grow more spiritual, first reality, then fancy, now pure spirit; a beautiful woman, a mystical nymph, a canonised soul. How was this to end? Perhaps I was ultimately designed for angelic discourse, perhaps I might mount the skies with the presiding essence of a star' (I, xiii, p. 48). Disraeli understands that Contarini's idealised quest relates to his adolescent sexuality. When Contarini's imaginative life virtually displaces his actual one, we see the parallel to Disraeli's own imaginative activity at the time he created *Contarini Fleming* and *Alroy*: 'I had now so completely a command of my system of abstraction that, while my eye apparently was employed and interested with my allotted page, I, in fact, perceived nothing but my visionary nymph' (I, vi, p. 21).

His father gives him practical advice on how to make a political career. Guided by this rather cynical advice, Contarini flourishes in public life until he meets Christiana, the woman who as an adolescent was the first person to understand his imaginative flights and who was an important catalyst for the growth during his childhood of his imaginative and poetic powers. As a child he 'would communicate to her in confidence all my secret sources of pleasure, and [explain] how I had turned common places into enchanted regions, where I could fly for refuge. . . . Now I had indeed a princess. Strolling with her, the berceau was still more like a forest, and the solace of the hermit's cell still more refreshing' (I, iv, p. 12). Years later, seeing her again has the kind of purifying effect that thinking of May Dacre has on the young Duke, and makes him believe that his political career has been a betrayal of his better self: 'I recoiled with disgust from the thought of my present life; I flew back with rapture to my old aspirations. . . . It was the innocence of Christiana that exercised over me a spell so potent. Her unsophisticated heart awoke in me a passion for the natural and the pure' (II, xii, p. 166). In a surge of creative energy, Contarini produces *Manstein*, whose subject and reception parallel those of Disraeli's *Vivian Grey*. Contarini no sooner scores a triumph at a conference of European statesmen and has his father predict he will be 'Prime Minister' or 'perhaps something greater', than he is exposed as the anonymous author of *Manstein*, which like *Vivian Grey* was taken by everyone as a *roman à clef*. He commits himself to a career as an author, and leaves a country whose society he now despises, determined to re-educate himself to 'principles of genuine morality' (II, xv, p. 187). When he reaches Venice, he falls in love with Alceste, the last of the Contarini line. Although she is betrothed to her cousin, he elopes with her. They live an idyllic life in Crete until Alceste dies while giving birth to a still-born child. Despairing, he embarks on a long journey in which he observes different customs, until finally he is called back to his home by his father's death. As the novel ends, he has withdrawn to private life on an estate in Naples which he has purchased with his inheritance, and dedicated himself to 'the study and the creation of the beautiful'. But mirroring his creator's own ambivalence to an artistic career, he expresses his devotion to the welfare and 'political regeneration' of his country and longs to play a public role again. The novel that Disraeli regarded as 'a development of my poetic character' actually shows a progress from the title character's dreams to his actual experience and from his self-interested political ambition to mature political ideals that place the nation's welfare first.

In *Contarini Fleming*, Disraeli divides himself into two characters: Contarini, the imaginative man who responds to impulses, passions, and unacknowledged psychic needs, and Contarini's father, Baron Fleming, the pragmatic, rational self who commits himself to public affairs despite his cynical view of mankind. Like Beckendorff, Baron Fleming is a benevolent Machiavellian who 'believed all to depend upon the influence of individual character. He required men not to think but to act, not to examine but to obey; and, animating their brute force with his own intelligence, he found the success, which he believed could never be attained by the rational conduct of an enlightened people' (I, xxi, pp. 96–97). If Disraeli objectified his imagination in the son, he transferred his will for power to the father. He himself believed in the ability of a forceful individual to shape his own destiny and the course of external events.

Disraeli's political philosophy was often based less upon principles than upon the belief that he could act in the best interest of those less perspicacious, intelligent and informed than himself. He believed that the 'natural aristocracy' of ability had the responsibility to lead and to do so in ways that served the interests of the entire people rather than the special interests of privileged classes. His portrait of Contarini's father is almost prophetic of the kinds of things that were later written of Disraeli himself after he emerged as a commanding political figure:

> His character . . . was perhaps inscrutable. . . . His talents were of high order, and their exercise alone had occasioned his rise in a country in which he had no interest and no connexions. . . . He respected the institutions of his country, because they existed, and

> because experience proved that under their influence the natives had become more powerful machines. . . . His practice of politics was compressed in two words: subtlety and force. (I, xxi, p. 96)

Even his public manner anticipates the figure that Disraeli was to cut in society:

> He was sumptuous in his habits. . . . Perhaps he affected gallantry, because he was deeply impressed with the influence of women both upon public and upon private opinion. . . . He . . . never lost his self-possession, and never . . . displayed a spark of strong feeling. (I, xxi, p. 97)

Contarini's father vociferously opposes a poetic career and seems to scorn activities of the imagination. On his deathbed he reveals that he has immersed himself in politics to compensate for emotional setbacks; he writes his son that he had been a poet and a romantic soul, but had suffered so much from his poetic aspirations that he had tried assiduously to deflect his son from repeating his frustrations and disappointments. Interestingly, despite his considerable success as a literary figure, Isaac D'Israeli encouraged his son to pursue law. Perhaps the father's position reflected Disraeli's own self-pity and disappointment at his failure to gain recognition for his literary achievement:

> Poets [are] the most miserable of their species. Depressed, doubtful, obscure, or involved in petty quarrels and petty persecutions; often unappreciated, utterly uninfluential, beggars, flatterers of men unworthy even of their recognition; what a train of disgusting incidents, what a record of degrading circumstances, is the life of a great poet! A man of great energies aspires that they should be felt in his lifetime, that his existence should be rendered more intensely vital by the constant consciousness of his multiplied and multiplying power. (II, ix, p. 155)

Disraeli used his fictional characters to create and test versions of his public and political identity. Fictional models such as the Baron and Winter – often not real men but idealised composites of qualities – may well have had as much a role in shaping his character as the real people he knew. Because of his father's antipathy to the imaginative life, Contarini turns to Winter, the artist, as a surrogate father. Winter is one of Disraeli's recurring wisdom figures (including such diverse characters as Beckendorff, Sidonia in *Coningsby* and *Tancred*, and Glastonbury in *Henrietta Temple*) whose role it is to counsel the protagonist. It is Winter who provides the sanction for his imaginative activity. Winter is at once an independent character and Contarini's own superego. He periodically re-appears to dissuade Contarini from self-indulgence and solipsism. Winter represents the position to which the speaker has evolved; hence he, like Sidonia, is static not dynamic. Aside from his lack of enthusiasm for Catholicism, his 'talismanic counsel' takes the form of abstract shibboleths which can be interpreted differently by each person: 'Be patient: Cherish hope. Read more: Ponder less. Nature is more powerful than education: Time will develop everything. Trust not overmuch in the blessed Magdalen: Learn to protect yourself' (I, xiii, p. 58). From a realistic standpoint, Contarini's dialogues with Winter may seem strained and bathetic unless they are understood as an exchange between Disraeli's adolescent ego and his mature conscience. As Contarini after losing his father savours the dreariness of his plight, Winter makes one of his characteristically unexpected appearances. To Contarini's complaint, 'The vanity of the present overpowers me', Winter responds: 'The period has arrived in your life, when you must renounce meditation. Action is now your part. Meditation is culture. It is well to think until a man has discovered his genius, and developed his faculties, but then let him put his intelligence in motion. Act, act, act; act without ceasing, and you will no longer talk of the vanity of life.' When Contarini asks, 'how am I to act?', Winter responds, 'Create. Man is made to create, from the poet to the potter' (p. 370). In 1832, this might have been Disraeli's advice to himself. Like Christiana and Alceste, Contarini's beloved countess, Winter appears when Contarini's psyche *requires* him. But, while Contarini's imagination seems to be able temporarily to transform optative into indicative, it cannot sustain its vision. Christiana eludes him, the Countess dies, and Winter can offer little consolation for that loss.

The plot dramatises, to quote from Contarini's concluding homily, that 'Circumstances are beyond the control of man; but his conduct is in his own power' (VII, ii, p. 373). But Disraeli really believed that circumstances could be significantly influenced by character. The novel's last paragraphs make clear that creativity is not necessarily limited to poetry and may include unspecified activities relating to 'the political regeneration of the country to which I am devoted' (VII, ii, p. 372). For Contarini that is Italy; but within the novel Disraeli uses Italy as a metaphor for England. Disraeli's prophetic tone is an outgrowth of the strain of moral seriousness that we have noted before. Nor must we forget that the 1830s were the period when Browning and Carlyle were self-appointed legislators for the world, a view that owed much to the influence of Shelley. Finally Disraeli understood that the Reform Act of 1832, which extended the franchise to the middle class, opened the door to people of ability and energy like himself.

The hortatory, even prophetic, ending has hardly been anticipated by what preceded it. Since Contarini has spent a good part of his young adulthood recovering from a physical breakdown that he does not understand and is currently living in solitude, the rhetoric of the final paragraphs seems unconvincing: 'When I examine the state of European society with the unimpassioned spirit which the philosopher can alone command, I perceive that it is in a state of transition, a state of transition from feudal to federal principles. This I conceive to be the sole and secret cause of all the convulsions that have occurred and are to occur' (VII, ii, p. 373). It is as if Disraeli could not allow his fictional character to foreclose the possibility of a political career. Contarini at this point is as far from being an 'impassioned spirit' as we could imagine, and nothing in the novel has prepared readers for his political observations. Given his chameleon-like nature, what assurances do we have that Contarini will not continue to evolve in unforeseen directions? And the ending is symptomatic of the structural flaws of this novel's later sections. What produces the unity of the first four Parts is the evolution of Contarini's imagination and character. But this unity gives way in Part V to a travelogue in which the speaker describes the customs and ceremonies of various cultures. To be sure, there is some anticipation of Disraeli's later political concerns, but the focus is too diffuse. Had he concentrated on the political aspects of the various cultures, the travel section might have been an indication of the growing range of Contarini's imagination and hence a justification for the final paragraphs.

Yet one aspect of Contarini's travels requires further discussion. Contarini, whose father was a Saxon, expresses a characteristic Disraeli theme when he speaks disparagingly of the Franks. He stresses their comparatively recent history as a civilised people and depicts them as visitors to the lands in which they are not the majority. His protagonists, from Contarini to Tancred to Lothair, are always more at home in the East than are other Europeans and find there a spiritual equilibrium that they lack in their own culture.

Disraeli took great pride in his Jewish heritage. He empathised with those who had a non-European heritage and resented the pretensions of those who thought that the Europeans were the fathers of civilisation. This reflected, no doubt, his own frustration at being patronised by Anglo-Saxons whom he regarded as only a few centuries removed from barbarism in contrast to the Semitic people's substantial contribution to western civilisation. At this stage of his career, the glorification of the Arabs was Disraeli's metaphor for illustrating the importance of the Jewish race. We must recall that in the 1830s Arab and Jew more or less peacefully co-existed in the Middle East. Since Disraeli regarded the Arabs as brothers of the Jews, his glorification of them disguised similar claims for the Jews. That the desert Bedouins approximate a utopia more than any other people will be clearer if we recall that Disraeli spoke of the Jews as a Bedouin race. The Bedouins, he wrote, 'combined primitive simplicity of habits with the refined feelings of civilisation, and . . . in a great degree, appeared to me to offer an evidence of that community of property and that equality of condition, which have hitherto proved the despair of European sages, and fed only the visions of their fanciful Utopias' (VI, iii, p. 350). Because Disraeli does not build on this concept it does not become part of the novel's imaginative world. Contarini's principles have no relation to the agrarian simplicity of the Bedouins.

The novel's style, like its structure, expresses the energy and spontaneity of Disraeli's imagination. Yet the passages already quoted from *Contarini* show that Disraeli's style is more poised and mature than in his first two novels. The prose is appropriate to the emotion described and reflects the subdued mood of a speaker looking back over his tumultuous life with a mixture of nostalgia and regret that is only occasionally interrupted by bursts of enthusiasm. Generally, the syntax is more logical, the diction more precise, the descriptions more restrained, and the rhetorical flights and climax in confusion are less frequent. However in the travelogue following Alceste's death, the prose and structure become looser.

Disraeli's handling of point of view is extremely complicated and sophisticated. Contarini's first-person monologue has a double focus. At times he consciously filters through his present consciousness his past thoughts and feelings. But at other times the past subsumes the present and we seem to get an unadulterated picture of his past self. For example when he recalls his idyllic life on Crete, he abandons himself to his memories. Even when his mind seems to be immersed in the past, he will often abruptly adjust his focus and disparagingly reject the past self that he had seemed to be sympathetically describing. Thus he concludes with bitter irony a chapter recalling how he modelled himself on his father and became a public servant in government: 'On the whole, I considered myself as one of the important personages of the country, possessing great talents, profound knowledge of men and affairs, and a perfect acquaintance with society. When I look back upon myself at this period, I have difficulty in conceiving a more unamiable character' (II, x, p. 159). Yet this quotation comes after a long passage in which Contarini almost *enjoys* recalling his cynical use of power and his sophistication: 'I recognised self-interest as the spring of all action. . . . The ardour and assiduity with which I fulfilled my duties and prosecuted my studies had rendered me, at the end of two years, a very skilful politician. . . . As a member of society I was entirely exempt from the unskilful affectation of my boyhood' (II, x, p. 158). Contarini's complex attitudes to his former ambition and *Realpolitik* reflect those of his creator. Because political ambitions burned within him even as he wrote *Contarini*, Disraeli is often sympathetic to Contarini's father.

Disraeli's own ambiguous vision of his younger self informs his attitude to Contarini. For example, in *Vivian Grey*, he rejected the over-reaching self who had become involved with the machinations of *The Representative*. But time has mellowed his view of that episode, and his self-denigration of his former self now lacks authenticity. He is sympathetic to the young man whose conflicts mime his own. While one aspect of Contarini demands the intensity and solitude of the life of poetry, the other prefers the excitement and ego-gratification of a life of action. Alternately and sometimes simultaneously Contarini expresses these contradictory selves. No sooner does he make a decision in one direction than he turns upon himself and rebukes himself for the life he is leading. His disdain of his former self is a characteristic of Vivian Grey, the young Duke, Alroy, and Disraeli himself.

Contarini, then, gives Disraeli a chance to objectify not only the emotions and feelings sanctioned by society, but those egoistic, and sometimes lawless and unacknowledged, impulses that Disraeli perceived within all his characters, because he perceived them within himself: 'I laid it down as a principle, that all considerations must yield to the gratification of my ambition' (II, x, p. 158). Incidents such as the one in which he becomes the leader of a band of marauding student-robbers are objectifications of Disraeli's imagination, as well as sanctioned outlets for Disraeli's own forbidden impulses. Contarini's ability to sustain his role as leader after the others lose faith testifies to the intensity of the imagination of the Disraeli surrogate who, like a masterly actor, can give himself to a role completely. Disraeli took lessons from his characters. Dramatising Contarini's imaginative powers helped convince Disraeli that he could be Prime Minister while he was still a virtual unknown, and, once he entered Parliament, to discover the means of achieving that unlikely goal.

The novel is built upon the premise that is voiced to Contarini by the oracular figure Winter: 'Never apologize for showing feeling . . . when you do so you apologize for truth' (I, xiii, p. 52). Disraeli may have set the novel in Europe to place it in the tradition of European novels (including Goethe's *Werther* and *Wilhelm Meister* and the works of Chateaubriand and Senancour) where feeling has epistemological value as the avenue to truth. Indeed he may have tentatively modelled himself on Goethe who had recognised Disraeli's genius.[21] Disraeli implies that each man has the capacity to discover his own truth by means of experience, if he is aided by an active imagination. Speaking through Contarini, Disraeli reaffirms the Romantic view that a major source of knowledge is an individual's experience; Truth is not in the world outside, but within the self:

> I am desirous of writing a book which shall be all truth; a work of which the passion, the thought, the action, and even the style, should spring from my own experience of feeling, from the meditations of my own intellect, from my own observation of incident, from my own study of the genius of expression. . . . When I search into my own breast, and trace the development of my own intellect, and the formation of my own character, all is light and order. The luminous succeeds to the obscure, the certain to the doubtful, the intelligent to the illogical, the practical to the impossible, and I experience all that refined and ennobling satisfaction that we derive from the discovery of truth, and the contemplation of nature. (I, i, p. 3)

Contarini's therapeutic and expressive theory of art shows a rare but acute recognition on Disraeli's part of the reasons he wrote fiction. Fiction became for Disraeli the means of ordering and controlling his personality. As he wrote, he rescued what he believed were his real values and emotions from a host of contradictory roles he played as political aspirant, dandy, scandalous novelist, Byronic iconoclast – to say nothing of his private relationships.

V

Alroy is Disraeli's ultimate heroic fantasy. He uses the figure of the twelfth-century Jewish Prince, Alroy, as the basis for a tale of Jewish conquest and empire. Disraeli found the medieval world in which Alroy lived an apt model for some of his own values. He saw in that world an emphasis on imagination, emotion and tradition; respect for political and social hierarchies; and a vital spiritual life. *Alroy* anticipates Disraeli's attraction for the Middle Ages in Young England. Writing of the flowering of medieval Jewry under Alroy enabled him to express his opposition to rationalism and utilitarianism.

In fact, the historic Alroy was a self-appointed messiah in Kurdistan during a period of severe tribulation and unusual suffering for the Jews.[22] Alroy's father claimed he was Elijah and that his son was the Messiah. Although his actual name was Menahem, young Alroy took the name David, the appropriate name for a king of the Jews, and promised to lead his followers to Jerusalem where he would be their king. Apparently learned in Jewish mysticism, Alroy managed to convince his followers that he could perform supernatural acts. While he scored some victories before he was murdered, probably by his father-in-law, his successes were hardly of the magnitude of his victories in Disraeli's romance.

Since completing *Vivian Grey*, Disraeli had been fascinated by Alroy, the Jew who had achieved power and prominence during Jewish captivity. But perhaps he needed the inspiration of his 1831 trip to Jerusalem to finish *Alroy*. Disraeli wrote in the Preface to *The Revolutionary Epick* (1834) that the purpose of *Alroy* was 'the celebration of a gorgeous incident in the annals of that sacred and romantic people from whom I derive my blood and name'.[23] Undoubtedly the tale of a Jew becoming the most powerful man in an alien land appealed to Disraeli, who at the age of twenty-nine had not yet made his political or artistic reputation. Indeed David Alroy's first name evokes visions of the David and Goliath legend which embodies another victory for a Jewish underdog. Disraeli uses the factual Alroy as a basis for his romance, but he extends Alroy's power and prowess and introduces supernatural machinery and ersatz Cabalistic lore and ritual.

Alroy represents Disraeli's own dreams of personal heroism and political power in the alien British culture. *Alroy* embodies not only his concept of himself as a potential leader, but his notion that the nation requires strong, visionary leaders who are true to its traditional manners and customs. Criticising Peel, he wrote, 'My conception of a great statesman is one who represents a great idea – an idea which may lead him to power; an idea with which he may identify himself; an idea which he may develop; an idea which he may and can impress on the mind and conscience of a nation.'[24] He felt that some men were born to lead, and believed that, like Alroy, he was one of these.

Doubtless Disraeli's journey to Jerusalem stimulated his fantasies of revived Jewish hegemony. Moreover, he believed that the Jews are not only an especially gifted race but the most aristocratic of races.[25] He also believed that the Jewish race is the source of all that is spiritual in European civilisation, most notably Christianity. Disraeli's only historical romance, except for 'The Rise of Iskander' (1833), resulted from his desire to depict Jews on a heroic scale. But it also derives from the discrepancy between his aspirations and his position in the early 1830s. In Alroy's hyperbolic self-dramatisation is the thinly disguised voice of the young frustrated Disraeli who has not yet begun to fulfil the 'ideal ambition' of which he wrote in his diary. Yet with typical Disraelian emotional resilience, Alroy's early self-pity and *ennui* give way to the vision of a transformation of his condition: 'I linger in this shadowy life, and feed on silent images which no eye but mine can gaze upon, till at length they are invested with all the terrible circumstance of life, and breathe, and act, and form a stirring world of fate and beauty, time, and death, and glory' (I, i, p. 8).

As the romance opens, Alroy is lost in despair and self-pity because both he and his people pay tribute to the Moslem Caliph: 'I know not what I feel, yet what I feel is madness. Thus to be is not to live, if life be what I sometimes dream, and dare to think it might be. To breathe, to feed, to sleep, to wake and breathe again, again to feel existence without hope; if this be life, why then these brooding thoughts that whisper death were better?' (I, i, p. 8). But the assault of the Moslem Lord Alschiroch upon Alroy's sister Miriam arouses him to action and he kills the Lord. As he sleeps 'dreaming of noble purposes and mighty hopes', Miriam awakes him and warns him that he must flee his home and the wrath of the Moslems. He makes his way to Jabaster who recognises him as 'the only hope of Israel' (III, i, p. 28). Alroy dreams that he has been anointed by the Lord to lead the

Jews out of Captivity to their chosen land, Jerusalem. Jabaster tells him that the Cabala insists he must get the sceptre of Solomon before he can free the Jews: 'None shall rise to free us, until, alone and unassisted, he have gained the sceptre which Solomon of old wielded within his cedar palaces' (III, iii, p. 33). Alroy undertakes a traditional romance quest, including visions, mysterious appearances and disappearances, and encounters with spirits, before receiving the sceptre from Solomon's own hand – only to see the King immediately disappear and to find himself transported once again to the company of Jabaster. Aided by Jabaster and the divinely inspired prophetess Esther, he begins to triumph. Beginning with a small band, he scores victory after victory and gradually conquers Bagdad. But at the height of his powers he falls in love with the Caliph's daughter, Princess Schirene, and betrays his mission by marrying her and not continuing to Jerusalem. Jabaster opposes the marriage and his decision to remain as Caliph of Bagdad as a betrayal of his commitment to Jewish customs and traditions. Jabaster argues for 'a national existence' and for re-establishing 'our beauteous country, our holy creed, our simple manners, and our ancient customs' (VIII, vi, p. 153), a position that looks forward to the traditionalism of Disraeli's Young England movement and the concept of a nation that dominated his thinking when in office.

When Alroy starts to enjoy his power and to savour his prominence, his visions and prophetic dreams cease and his decline begins. Eventually he loses a vital battle to the Karasmians and re-enters Bagdad as a captive. Disraeli's implication is that arrogance and self-conceit are incompatible with imaginative activity. The significance and frequency of his imaginative experience decline as he forgets God's command and marries Schirene; the alliance with a Gentile ironically fulfils his identity as a second Solomon. When Alroy tells Jabaster, 'We must leave off dreaming', he renounces imagination, the very quality that has given him the capacity to achieve greatness. Alroy's rationalism and worldliness betray the dream of rebuilding the temple which was the catalyst for his heroic activity. Alroy's apostasy begins when he belittles Jerusalem and when he dismisses the Prophetess Esther as a 'quaint fanatic' after she counsels him not to enter Bagdad, which she calls Babylon. He becomes concerned with secular matters, such as the need for a 'marshal of the palace', the position to which he appoints Honain (VIII, i, p. 141). He is captivated by the princess, whom he had previously rejected when he had first been tempted by her. At this point we recall not only the prophetess' denunciation of Bagdad, but Alroy's own words to Honain: 'I fly from this dangerous city upon [God's] business, which I have too much neglected' (V, vi, p. 74). Speaking the language of courtly love, he puts Schirene before his love for God, and renounces his heritage: 'If the deep devotion of the soul of Alroy be deemed an offering meet for the shrine of thy surpassing loveliness, I worship thee, Schirene, I worship thee, I worship thee!' (VIII, iv, p. 148).

In *Alroy* the evolving pattern of events and circumstances depends upon Alroy's moral health, whereas we have seen in *Contarini Fleming* that the character's visions and dreams, and on occasion actual events, depend on his psychological life. Alroy's moral status *determines* the action. Such a pattern, in which a man's behaviour shapes the world, enables Disraeli to reconcile the conflict between his own poetic and political ambition. For example, when Alroy has the confidence to restore Israel's glory, he has the vision in which he fulfils his quest for the sceptre of Solomon. Or, when the trumpet sounds to signal the time for Alroy's trial, Miriam in response to his disgrace dies. The Jewish participants in the alliance that overthrew Alroy are absent from the denouement, as if by their part in Alroy's overthrow they deserve to be discarded from the romance.

As with Contarini, Alroy's visionary experience occurs in times of heightened awareness, but these states cease to occur during his complacent rule of Babylon. Alroy regains the capacity to experience the spectre of Jabaster when he recognises the vulnerability of his actual situation prior to the climactic battle: 'I feel more like a doomed and desperate renegade than a young hero on the verge of battle, flushed with the memory of unbroken triumphs!' (X, x, p. 202). Alroy's imaginative powers recover as he begins to acknowledge his shortcomings and his unjust treatment of the prophetess and Jabaster. Before his battle with the rebels, he realises: 'I am not what I was. I have little faith. All about me seems changed, and dull, and grown mechanical' (X, v, p. 202). Even though he knows Jabaster's ghost is summoning him to his doom, he seems to welcome his presence; Alroy knowingly accepts as his retribution a pattern of events which will fulfil the prophecy of his own destruction: 'A rushing destiny carries me onward. I cannot stem the course, nor guide the vessel' (X, x, p. 211). But at the height of his military successes, when he feels fulfilled as a public man, his imagination becomes less active because he has deviated from his purposes. At this point he condemns Abidan, one of his most loyal, if zealous, lieutenants as a 'dreamer' and rejects the prophetess Esther's visions (VIII, i, p. 139). When Alroy becomes a man of the world and forswears his imaginative experiences, he is already on the road to his undoing. His success derives from his faith, from his idealism, and from his powers of imagination that enable him to hear the Daughter of the Voice and to dream of Afrites. Condemning Abidan is tantamount to rejecting his former self. Gradually he ceases to be the Prince of Captivity, not because he fulfils his holy purpose of rebuilding the temple and restoring the Jews to Jerusalem, but because he becomes Caliph. Although Alroy's religious faith had been his best political guide, he abandons that and begins to rely on reason:

> The world is mine: and shall I yield the prize, the universal and heroic prize, to realize the dull tradition of some dreaming priest, and consecrate a legend? He conquered Asia, and he built the temple. . . . Is the Lord of hosts so slight a God, that we must place a barrier to His sovereignty, and fix the boundaries of Omnipotence between the Jordan and the Lebanon? . . . Well, I am clearly summoned, I am the Lord's servant, not Jabaster's. Let me make His worship universal as His power; and where's the priest shall dare impugn my faith, because His altars smoke on other hills than those of Judah? (VIII, i, p. 141)

Alroy's pride makes him believe that he is entitled to reinterpret the Lord's calling. He relies on reason rather than inspiration; sophistry displaces imagination. At least through the Young England period, Disraeli believed in the imagination as a necessary guide to political wisdom. The limitations of reason are illustrated in *Popanilla* (1828), Disraeli's satire of utilitarianism.

Jabaster and Abidan are dedicated to ideological purity whatever the consequences. In the name of theocracy, they reject Alroy's power. Yet in their conspiracy against their leader, we may see Disraeli's impatience with those who would limit the English King's power. Later, this attitude became part of his coherent political philosophy in *A Vindication of the English Constitution* (1835). Abidan's justification for regicide is a deliberate satire of Cromwell's views: 'King! Why what's a king? Why should one man break the equal sanctity of our chosen race? Is their blood purer than our own? We are all the seed of Abraham' (IX, i, pp. 172–3). Just as Honain and Schirene tempt Alroy, Abidan tempts Jabaster by appealing to his vanity: 'Thou ne'er didst err, but when thou placedst a crown upon this haughty stripling. . . . 'Twas thy mind inspired the deed. And now he is king; and now Jabaster, the very soul of Israel, who should be our Judge and leader, Jabaster trembles in disgrace . . .' (IX, i, p. 173). Disraeli implies that the zealotry of Jabaster, who would massacre Moslems, is both inhumane and misguided, if for no other reason than that the wheel of fortune has a way of turning. Significantly, Alroy later recalls his own gentle rule as Caliph, when he is being subjected to cruel punishment; because he refuses to forswear his faith and insists that he is the Lord's anointed, he dies a martyr's death. Perhaps Disraeli wished to remind his primarily Christian audience that the Jews had a long tradition of being the victims of persecution.

Disraeli is ambivalent to Honain, Jabaster's brother who has achieved prominence under the Caliph's rule and who again is serving Alroy's conquerors. On one hand, Honain's equivocation represents a temptation that Alroy must reject. On the other hand, he is the ultimate pragmatist who counsels compromise in contrast to his brother's ideological purity. His brother's polar opposite, he lives by his own resources and eschews commitment to principles. As such, he is an heir to Beckendorff and Contarini's father, whose creeds he suggests when he asserts, 'We make our fortunes, and we call them Fate' (V, vi, p. 73). Honain survives three Caliphs because his own welfare is at the centre of his value system. The very moment that Alroy rejects Jabaster he acknowledges the abilities of Honain, the man who lives by his wits: 'I must see Honain. That man has a great mind. He alone can comprehend my purpose' (VIII, i, p. 141). Honain always counsels worldliness and, after Alroy's capture, compromise. He is an example of the apostate Jew who has made his way in the world. Perhaps he is a projection of Disraeli's view of his own father's apostasy. Honain may also reflect Disraeli's own troubled response to his Jewish roots.

If Contarini vacillates erratically between imagination and action, Disraeli shows in *Alroy* that the life of action is not incompatible with the imaginative life. For Alroy's political success is dependent upon visions that show how a life of action need not exclude poetic and imaginative impulses. Alroy uses his imagination in the service of his political goals. For example, the catalyst for his original act of rebellion is his insight that, as 'the descendant of sacred kings', he is not suited for a life of activity (I, i, p. 9). His imagination creates the fiction of Jewish and personal glory. Killing the city governor Alschiroch who harassed his sister (his alter ego throughout the novel) is the necessary heroic action which takes him from the imaginative world into the public world.

That sexual motives play an important part in *Alroy* and often displace heroic and public motives is an indication of Disraeli's worldliness and refusal to compromise his own complex vision of mankind's motives and needs for the sake of the character who embodies his fantasy of Jewish eminence. Alroy's conduct, including his tolerance of Moslem influence in his council, is shaped by his erotic interest in Schirene, the Gentile princess of Bagdad whom he eventually marries. The prophetess's real motive for wishing to murder Alroy is not so much ideological purity as sexual jealousy. As she watches Alroy sleep, her monologue begins with the indictment that he is 'a tyrant and a traitor' who has betrayed God's trust. But like all those who *think* that they act under God's auspices – Alroy, Abidan, Jabaster – she is not without pathetically human feelings and failings: 'Hush my heart, and let thy secret lie hid in the charnel-house of crushed affections. Hard is the lot of woman: to love and to conceal is our sharp doom! O bitter life! O most unnatural lot! Man made society, and made us slaves. And so we droop and die, or else take refuge in idle fantasies, to which we bring the fervour that is meant for nobler ends' (IX, v, p. 184).

Disraeli wants to create a context where the marvellous is possible. Moreover, he wishes to present himself as an original artist and to flout conventional expectations as to what a work of prose fiction should be. His use of rhythm and rhyme is part of his rebellion against artistic captivity, a captivity created by standards he did not recognise and by what he felt was failure to appreciate his genius. In the original preface to *Alroy*, Disraeli stressed the genius of his achievement, particularly the prose poetry. *Alroy* is written in a prophetic tone and biblical rhythms as if Disraeli were proposing this as his contribution to Jewish lore. The fastidious notes are in the tradition of talmudic learning that addresses texts as sacred and values scholarship as homage to God. That *Alroy* is written in metrical prose punctuated by what Disraeli called 'occasional bursts of lyric melody', is the primary reason for the remoteness of its prose from colloquial English.[26] Lyric interludes, sometimes in rhyme, certainly contribute to Disraeli's efforts to create an ersatz orientalism based on artifice rather than mimesis: 'The carol of a lonely bird singing in the wilderness! A lonely bird that sings with glee! Sunny and sweet, and light and clear, its airy notes float through the sky, and trill with innocent revelry' (II, iv, p. 24). But the stylised dialogue, the vatic tone accompanying the spare plot, the supernatural machinery, the bizarre reversals of fortune, and the hyperbolic descriptions of setting all contribute to astonish the normal expectations that a reader brings to prose fiction. Thus the 'wondrous' tale describes not only Alroy's conquests, but the tale itself with its remarkable style and tone. While the style deprives us of Disraeli's ironic wit and playful vivacity, the taut symmetrical plot, which accelerates as it reaches Alroy's demise, shows progression in Disraeli's mastery of narrative form. The subject is hardly conducive to his exuberant self-mockery or boisterous digressions. But, although the author takes himself as seriously as he ever does in any of his prose fiction, Disraeli's propensity for elaborate description, which was so much of the fun of the first novels, finds an outlet in the wonders of life in Bagdad, as in the following passage:

> The line of domestics at the end of the apartment opened, and a body of slaves advanced, carrying trays of ivory and gold, and ebony and silver, covered with the choicest dainties, curiously prepared. These were in turn offered to the Caliph and the Sultana by their surrounding attendants. The Princess accepted a spoon made of a single pearl, the long, thin golden handle of which was studded with rubies, and condescended to partake of some saffron soup, of which she was fond. Afterwards she regaled herself with the breast of a cygnet stuffed with almonds, and stewed with violets and cream. . . . Her attention was then engaged with a dish of those delicate ortolans that feed upon the vine-leaves of Schiraz, and with which the Governor of Nishabur took especial care that she should be well provided. Tearing the delicate birds to pieces with the still more delicate fingers, she insisted upon feeding Alroy, who of course yielded to her solicitations. (IX, ii, p. 177)

Disraeli wanted to establish the authenticity of his wondrous tale. For that reason he created as his editor-speaker a Jewish historian and scholar. But he must have known that very few readers would discover that he had taken liberties with the Alroy legend and really knew only scattered bits and snips of the Cabala tradition. One wonders whether the notes are in part an elaborate joke at the expense of readers who would take the editor and themselves too seriously and accept what is often mumbo jumbo. Is there not a note of dead pan humour in the following from the 1845 preface: 'With regard to the supernatural machinery of this romance, it is Cabalistical and correct'? Disraeli must have known that given the multiple and contradictory sources, it is impossible to be correct about either the legend of Alroy or the Cabala. According to the *Encyclopedia Judaica*, the Cabala is a general term for 'esoterical teachings of Judaism and for Jewish mysticism', but there is no accepted and correct 'version'. And the factual record of Alroy and his movement is, according to the same source, 'contradictory and tendentious'.[27]

Interweaving personal recollections of the East with informed if rather abstruse knowledge of Jewish lore, the notes mediate between the text and the audience. The notes become part of the reading experience and give *Alroy* an authenticity as Jewish myth that it lacks as personal fantasy. *Alroy* fuses the myths of the Chosen People, of return to the homeland, and of the long awaited Messiah. As is appropriate in Judaic tradition, Alroy turns out to be a heroic man, but not without human limitations. His demise may be Disraeli's unconscious affirmation of the Jewish tradition that the Messiah has not yet come to redeem mankind. When Jabaster rebukes him for not following his mission ('you may be King of Bagdad, but you cannot, at the same time, be a Jew',) a spirit shrieks 'Mene, Mene, Tekel, Upharsin', the words that Daniel interprets upon the wall to mean that God had weighed Belshazzar and his kingdom and found them wanting (VIII, vi, pp. 156–7). Significantly, Alroy regains the Jewish title, Prince of Captivity, after he is overthrown as Caliph. In his final suffering and humility, he has achieved the stature that the Jewish exiled Prince, Disraeli's metaphor for himself, deserves.

The Jewish desire for a Messiah is not finally fulfilled, but Alroy has significance for others, and particularly other Jews, as a historical figure. Miriam's epitaph suggests Carlyle's notion of the value of an heroic figure: 'Great deeds are great legacies, and work with wondrous usury. By what Man has done, we learn what Man can do; and gauge the power and prospects of our race. . . . The memory of great actions never dies' (X, xix, p. 241). Disraeli the imaginative poet is the heir to Alroy the imaginative man. Perhaps, by telling his story of the Jew who rose to prominence in a foreign land, it became more plausible to imagine himself as a political leader. But if Alroy is an objectification of Disraeli's ambition, does he not also reflect Disraeli's anxieties and doubts, specifically his fear of his own sensual weakness and a certain paranoia about betrayal? Perhaps he wondered whether, like Daniel and Alroy, he would be found wanting when his opportunity came.

Yet *Alroy* indicates Disraeli's commitment to his Jewish heritage.

His surrogate, the narrator, glories in the Jewish victories and in the triumph of the Prince of Captivity over his oppressors. Disraeli's notes, which are a fundamental part of reading Alroy, show not only his knowledge of Jewish customs, but his wide reading in Jewish studies. His notes not only demonstrate both to *himself* and his readers that he has the intellectual and racial credentials to narrate Jewish history and legend, but they give us the perspective of a Jewish scholar who is trying to provide an authoritative edition of the Alroy legend. Indeed, Miriam had anticipated the possibility of such a poet-editor: 'Perchance some poet, in some distant age, within whose veins our sacred blood may flow, his fancy fired by the national theme, may strike his harp to Alroy's wild career, and consecrate a name too long forgotten?' (X, xix, p. 241).

VI

Disraeli's first four novels mime his psyche. His emotions, fantasies, aspirations and anxieties become fictional names, personalities and actions. These novels are moral parables told by himself for himself about ambitious egoists. He dramatises the political rise and setback of an unscrupulous young man; the moral malaise and subsequent enlightenment of a young English Duke; the flamboyant career of a young Count who is torn between politics and poetry as well as between feeling and intellect; and finally the biography of Alroy, a Jewish Prince who conquers much of Asia only to lose his kingdom and his life as he compromises his principles.

Disraeli uses his early novels, in particular *Alroy* and *Contarini*, as a means of controlling himself, of understanding himself, and of exorcising flamboyant postures and forbidden emotions. For example, Alroy reflects Disraeli's fantasies of conquest and his will to power. In his early novels, the distinction between the external events and the interior visions of the title character blurs. The reason is that both are reflections of the author's subjective life and both are dramatisations of his evolving imagination. In *Alroy*, both the divine machinery and the title character's adventures are the metaphorical vehicles for Disraeli's attitudes and states of mind, and have as little to do with the phenomenal world as William Blake's prophecies.

Like Oscar Wilde, Disraeli used his literary creations as masks to disguise his wounded sensibilities and as devices to objectify aspects of himself that society would not tolerate. In his fiction, he freed himself from conventions and traditions, from priggishness and condescension, and found room for his fantasies. He discovered an alternative to the turmoil of his personal life in the *act* of creating the imagined worlds of his novels. But Disraeli's early novels are more than the creations of an egoistic, ambitious, but frustrated young man who found a temporary outlet for his imagination in the fictions he created. For the roles one imagines are as indicative of one's real self as supposedly 'sincere' moments, intense personal relationships, or daily routines. In the early novels the title character and the narrator represent the two sides of Disraeli. While the title character embodies Byronic fantasies of passionate love, heroism and rebellion against society's values, the narrator judges him according to standards that represent traditional values and the community's interest. In the first four books of *Vivian Grey* and in *The Young Duke*, the narrator represents the political and social health of England; in *Alroy*, the narrator speaks for the interest of the Jews even after Alroy has betrayed them. In *Contarini* and in the later books of *Vivian Grey*, Disraeli speaks for a commitment to public life based on ideals rather than cynical self-interest.

With some justification, one could schematise the four early novels according to the following formula: each contains a version of the bold, impetuous independent self that Disraeli wished to be, and each is narrated by the mature, controlled voice that Disraeli desired to become. The major characters – Vivian Grey, the young Duke, Contarini Fleming, Alroy – are projections of a passionate, intuitive self that Disraeli knew he must put behind him. In these novels the narrator functions as the major character's superego; he censors that figure's bold, impulsive behaviour even as he reports it. The title figure's experience ranges from triumph to immoderate ill fortune; his emotions vacillate erratically from exaltation to suffering and despair. Characteristically, he uses his imagination to create an heroic version of himself and spends his energies trying to live up to that version. But events do not sustain this idealised self. Gradually his self-image is reduced to correspond to the more human and fallible impression that the narrator has presented to the reader. But such a formulation ignores Disraeli's frequent disregard of fictional form and his unconscious resistance to fictional conventions and narrative unity.

Recalling Boswell's famous statement in *The London Journal*, 'A man cannot know himself better than by attending to the feelings of his heart and to his external actions', Martin Price has observed: 'This movement from immersion to reflection, from inside to outside, from subject to object, from I to he, becomes a problem of characterisation'.[28] But in his early novels Disraeli could never complete that movement. Thus these novels, while often quite elegant, sometimes seem inchoate bursts of energy from their creator, rather than polished works of art. As the voice of the narrator, Disraeli is a ubiquitous presence pervading and often overwhelming his nominal subject. The distance between author and protagonist often threatens to disintegrate because Disraeli cannot separate himself from his created world. Thus although the narrator and protagonist are quite separate from each other, as they are in all but *Contarini Fleming*, the author's voice at times subsumes both figures.

Disraeli's career as artist and politician should be seen in the context of the Romantic movement. As Harold Fisch has remarked,

> Insofar as his novels are the expression of his personal life, his feelings, his scarcely avowed hidden ideals, he achieves an appropriately resonant statement. His novels have the subtle egoism of all true romantics, of Shelley, of Wordsworth, of Milton. His subject is himself: he is Coningsby; he is Contarini Fleming; he is Alroy; he is Tancred; and he is the Wandering Jew, Sidonia. From these varied characters we are able to reconstruct the inner vision of Disraeli, the rich landscape of his dreams, his irrepressible vision of grandeur, of power, but power used for glorious and elevating ends. . . . Disraeli is certainly an egoist, but if that means that he is impelled by a sense of personal dedication, of election, of being favoured and gifted to an almost unlimited degree, and of being charged with grand tasks and opportunities, then it is the sort of egoism which finds its parallel in the lives of the great romantic poets and dreamers, of Milton, Wordsworth and Shelley.[29]

In the early novels, he could be the Romantic figure that tantalised his imagination without sacrificing the public image that he wished to cultivate. To be sure, he might dress unconventionally and play the dandy, but that kind of socially sanctioned rebelliousness was different in kind rather than degree from the imagined social outlawry of Vivian Grey, Alroy and Contarini.

Contarini Fleming and *Alroy* are meant as visions rather than restatements of known truths. Disraeli tries to extend into prose the fusion of politics and philosophy – as well as the range and imaginative energy – of the Miltonic epic and the Romantic masterworks such as Blake's prophecies, *The Prelude*, *Prometheus Unbound* and *Don Juan*. While Disraeli's works at times seem bathetic when viewed in the context of this tradition, there can be no doubt that he saw himself in the line of Romantic visionaries that M. H. Abrams has described:

> The Romantics, then, often spoke confidently as elected members of what Harold Bloom calls 'The Visionary Company', the inspired line of singers from the prophets of the Old and New Testament, through Dante, Spenser, and above all Milton. . . . Whatever the form, the Romantic Bard is one 'who present, past and future sees'; so that in dealing with current affairs his procedure is often panoramic, his stage cosmic, his agents quasi-mythological, and logic of events apocalyptic. Typically this mode of Romantic vision fuses history, politics, philosophy and religion into one grand design, by asserting Providence – or some form of natural teleology – to operate in the seeming chaos of human history so as to effect from present evil a greater good.[30]

In the early novels, Disraeli tentatively posits the movement towards the grand design, and shows how a man's personal destiny can be woven into the fabric of a nation's destiny. But, perhaps because of his own self-doubts and exclusion from public position, only *The Young Duke* even remotely sustains that vision. Disraeli's inability to sustain his fantasy of heroic accomplishment, combined with his realisation that he could use his imagination and emotional energy in the world of politics, may have relegated novel writing to a secondary position. Disappointed with the reception accorded to his first four novels and his satire *Popanilla*, he turned to poetry and began to write what he believed would be the major epic for his age, entitled *The Revolutionary Epick* (1834). He believed that this poem would reflect the intellectual and cultural texture of his age in the way that *The Aeneid* and *Paradise Lost* reflected the Augustan Age and the Reformation. Because of its chilly reception he abandoned it after the third Book. Later in the decade he returned to novel writing and produced *Henrietta Temple* (1836) and *Venetia* (1837) at a time when he required an outlet for his passions and frustrations, and, not so incidentally, when financial exigency required it.

2 From Immersion to Reflection: Romance and Realism in *Henrietta Temple* and *Venetia*

I

The only book-length critical study of Disraeli's novels, Richard A. Levine's *Benjamin Disraeli*, criticises *Henrietta Temple* (1836) and *Venetia* (1837) because of their supposed objectivity: 'In the final analysis, however, [*Henrietta Temple*] is neither typical nor meaningful in Disraeli's canon; for it carries within it few ideas or authorial observations, and Disraeli's fundamental interests for us are as a novelist of ideas and as a writer of personal involvement and observation. In *Henrietta Temple* and *Venetia*, Disraeli stands at some distance from his creations and produces two relatively impersonal works. His effectiveness for us is thereby lessened.'[1] My argument in this chapter will take issue with Levine's statement on a number of grounds: (i) *Venetia* and *Henrietta Temple* have important continuities with Disraeli's other work; (ii) the novels have thematic interest and aesthetic appeal apart from Disraeli's ideas; (iii) these middle novels do not suffer from the author having created more objective characters; and (iv) finally, although Disraeli does move, to recall Price's phrase, from immersion to reflection, these novels are hardly impersonal.

The family is the essential focus of Disraeli's middle period, particularly the way a child relates to his family history. The eighteenth-century novel's focus on the plight of orphans and disowned children may have provided Disraeli with a model. The early English novel is preoccupied with the relationship between fathers and sons, with the search of parents for real or putative children and vice versa, and with the plight of the homeless, rejected child. As political ideology and religious institutions failed to provide certainties, the English novel intensified its concern with nuances of family relationships, a concern which continues in Woolf, Lawrence and Joyce. One reason for the primacy of family relationships in the eighteenth- and nineteenth-century English novel may be the gradual diminishment of the English monarchy. Certainly nineteenth-century England's perception of the royal family as a kind of paradigmatic domestic institution gradually replaced the Renaissance concept that the king was God's representative on earth. Family values became an alternative to the primacy of church and Monarchy in the lives of individuals. As Walter Houghton has written in his chapter on 'Love' in *The Victorian Frame of Mind*, 'the sanctification of love and woman could rescue a worried Victorian from sliding into disbelief by reassuring him of a divine world, manifested here in the flesh, so to speak'.[2]

Throughout his career, Disraeli required private relations to balance his ambition. Once he attained office it was essential for him to go to Hughenden for rest and renewal. It may be that the emotional security of a womblike retreat to his wife and home was not only an alternative to political turmoil, but also compensation both for ambiguous national identity and for his apparently unsatisfactory relationship with his mother. As Blake notes, 'All his life he seems to be searching for a substitute for the mother who was somehow missing. His wife, his mistresses, his friends were almost always older women who could, or he hoped they could, supply that need'.[3] His quest for older, maternal women culminated in his marrying Mary Anne Lewis, a woman eleven years his senior.

In these novels, written during and subsequent to his affairs with older women, most notably Henrietta Sykes, Disraeli dramatises several variations of the relationship between parent and child. At this time, he was anxious to wrench himself free from financial dependence upon his father. Until he married in 1839, his father provided him with a centre of stability at crucial periods in his life, although neither his father nor his wife seems to have been a strong dominating figure. In the memoir which Disraeli prefaced to the 1848 edition of his father's *Curiosities of Literature*, he wrote: 'The philosophic sweetness of his disposition, the serenity of his lot, and the elevating nature of his pursuits, combined to enable him to pass through life without an evil act, almost without an evil thought'.[4] In *Venetia*, his narrator comments on the supremacy of parental love:

> All other intimacies, however ardent, are liable to cool; all other confidences, however unlimited, to be violated. . . . Love is a dream, and friendship a delusion. No wonder we grow callous; for how few have the opportunity of returning to the hearth which they have quitted in levity or thoughtless weariness, yet which alone is faithful to them; whose sweet affections require not the stimulus of prosperity or fame, the lure of accomplishments, or the tribute of flattery; but which are constant to us in distress, and console us even in disgrace. (I, xvii, p. 90)

Even if the passage was written at a time of disappointment with his former friend Benjamin Austen for haunting him about an unpaid debt, and with Henrietta Sykes for betraying his love, the passage accurately reflects Disraeli's views.[5]

A brief look at the plots of these novels will illustrate Disraeli's focus on family responsibility and heterosexual relationships. The historical sweep of the opening chapters may represent an unsuccessful attempt to make Ferdinand Armine's social and economic history typical of the history of the Catholic nobility in England. But the real subject is the redemptive possibilities of heterosexual passion for a potentially talented, but immature and irresponsible young man. As *Henrietta Temple* opens, Ferdinand Armine is the only child of parents whose family fortune is in decline. He had been educated by the family priest Glastonbury who obtains a commission for him in Malta. As the favourite of his maternal grandfather, Ferdinand expects to be heir to a considerable estate and on the basis of his expectations lives extravagantly. But when his grandfather dies, the fortune is left to the grand-daughter, Katherine Grandison. To redeem the family fortune, Ferdinand becomes engaged to Katherine, but after he returns home, he discovers the beautiful and gifted Henrietta Temple with whom he falls in love at first sight. Ferdinand asks her to keep their love a secret until he informs his parents, who are at Bath; Henrietta reluctantly agrees not to tell her father of their engagement until he returns. Of course, Ferdinand does not tell her that he is in fact engaged to two women. After three weeks, the Temples learn that Ferdinand has betrayed their trust and is engaged to Katherine.

Upon learning of Ferdinand's duplicity, Henrietta has a nervous collapse and goes to Italy to recover. There she meets and eventually becomes engaged to Lord Montfort, whose decorum and tact are in striking contrast to Ferdinand's passion. Ferdinand is befriended by Count Mirabel (a character based on Count D'Orsay, the famous dandy and a close friend of Disraeli) who helps Ferdinand woo and win Henrietta. Mirabel consoles Ferdinand when he suffers the ignominy of a sponging-house – and even raises the necessary funds to pay Ferdinand's debts, although by then Katherine has already learned of his plight and paid his release. When Montfort and Katherine discover their temperamental compatability, the obstacles to the marriage of Henrietta and Ferdinand dissolve. The novel concludes with both couples happily married.

Disraeli was in desperate financial straits when he wrote *Venetia*, in part because *Henrietta Temple*, although his most successful novel since *Vivian Grey*, did not produce anything like the revenue he required to pay his debts. He chose for his subjects England's most unconventional recent poetic geniuses, Shelley and Byron, because they gave him an opportunity to embody in fiction his pique that major artists, like himself, were unappreciated if not ostracised. Disraeli saw himself as heir to the tradition of genius which those figures represented to him. By creating fictional versions of Byron and Shelley, he was reaffirming his ties to the Romantic tradition. Because Shelley and Byron were both regarded as disreputable and immoral genuises by the early Victorian establishment, his choice of subject was both a ploy to attract a voyeuristic audience and a statement about the kind of imaginative and personal life that intrigued him. His major figures, Lord Cadurcis and Marmion Herbert, are modelled respectively on Byron and Shelley. (In the novel Shelley is a generation older, although he was actually three years younger.) The novel fuses the melodrama of the Gothic plot with Disraeli's intensifying interest in the inner workings of the psyche.

Deserted by her husband and living in self-imposed seclusion in Cherbury, Lady Annabel Herbert (modelled on Byron's wife who was called Annabelle) devotes her life to her child, Venetia. Cadurcis and his mother come to live at the nearby Abbey. Because his mother is emotionally erratic if not mentally ill, Cadurcis becomes increasingly dependent on the affection of Lady Annabel and Venetia. When his mother abuses him without provocation, he runs away, and during his flight, his mother dies of heart failure. Subsequently Cadurcis leaves the Abbey to continue his education. Only the local vicar, Dr Masham, knows the secret of Venetia's paternity or the reasons for her mother's seclusion. One day Venetia discovers that a closed-off room contains her father's portrait and his poems which she reads. In true Gothic fashion, she becomes ill; while delirious, she reveals to her mother what she has seen.

After a long absence and years without correspondence, Cadurcis returns and after renewing his acquaintance with Venetia, proclaims his love. But Venetia refuses, because she feels Cadurcis is not the equal to her father, whom she has apotheosised. After Venetia rejects him because of her devotion to her father and tells him that she would only 'unite [her] fate' with 'a great man; one with whose name the world rung; perhaps, like my father, a genius and a poet' (III, vii, p. 201), Cadurcis begins to emulate the career of her father as a social rebel and as a poet. He becomes a famous poet who is lionised by London society. He woos Venetia by praising her father in a poem, but Lady Annabel, fearing that her daughter will also be deserted by a poet who has become a public figure, now opposes the relationship. After Cadurcis fights a duel with the man with whose wife he has had an affair, he becomes a notorious character. No sooner does he write a volume which won him sympathy than 'he left his native shores in a blaze of glory, but with the accents of scorn still quivering on his lip' (IV, xix, 331). The scene shifts to Europe where not only Venetia and Cadurcis, but also Marmion and Lady Annabel are reunited. After a short period of bliss, Herbert and Cadurcis drown in a boating accident. Venetia returns to Cherbury, but eventually rejects the former celibate existence of her mother and marries Cadurcis's loyal if unexciting cousin, George.

In *Henrietta Temple* and *Venetia* Disraeli is not only more interested than he once was in the subtleties of private lives, and the way that the child is father to the man, but also in observing complex psychological problems. In contrast to his early novels, he is no longer preoccupied with projecting his own radically vacillating emotions into the psychological pattern of the protagonists. He understands how binding the maternal tie can be on a fatherless boy. In *Venetia*, Lord Cadurcis is profoundly affected by the death of his mother, no doubt in part because his departure, after she struck him, was the catalytic event that caused her death, but also because he instinctively understands that his mother's abusive behaviour was at odds with her intent. With a good deal of childish wisdom he understands that 'A mother is your friend as long as she lives; she cannot help being your friend' (I, xviii, p. 91). Yet such is his emotional need that he responds to Lady Annabel's surrogate mother role even while he regrets the loss of his own mother. Ferdinand Armine is torn between his family commitment and his personal emotional needs. The memory of his emotional separation from his mother when he joined the army has oedipal overtones. After he realises that he is passionately in love with Henrietta, he feels he has betrayed his mother by displacing her: 'Ah! he loves another woman better than his mother now. Nay, even a feeling of embarrassment and pain is associated with the recollection of that fond and elegant being, that he had recognised once as the model of all feminine perfection, and who had been to him so gentle and so devoted. He drives his mother from his thoughts' (III, i, p. 150). Ironically, his emotion is similar to Henrietta's guilt for loving someone other than her father. True, she feels bad that she cannot share her feelings with him, but her complex emotions seem to be a response to an incipient awareness that she plays more than a mere daughter's role in his life. Mr Temple wants to direct her choice, and when he does so he chooses a man who authenticates him, a man who is a younger version of himself, Lord Montfort, and who offers Henrietta the polish and elegance that she had found in her father. But Henrietta is drawn to Ferdinand's passion and spontaneity, qualities that her father lacks. She recollects her father in terms which recreate her astonishment and excitement, and which illustrate her unsuccessful effort to view her new emotions with detachment: 'She who had moved in the world so variously, who had received so much homage, and been accustomed from her childhood to all that is considered accomplished and fascinating in man, and had passed through the ordeal with a calm, clear spirit; behold, she is no longer the mistress of her thoughts and feelings; she had fallen before a glance, and yielded in an instant to a burning word!' (III, ii, p. 154). The last phrases underline the difference from her father's cool elegance. Venetia, like Ferdinand, must overcome a physical illness caused by emotional problems.

In these novels Disraeli becomes a defter psychologist which relates to his ability to maintain a clear distinction between himself and his characters. He is now concerned with the intricacies of behaviour in the world beyond himself. Such an instance is his striking portrait of the severely disturbed, although well-meaning mother of Cadurcis. Mrs Cadurcis is a character whose behaviour is controlled by atavistic passions and unacknowledged impulses that she cannot understand. When we realise that in 1836 Dickens had only just begun to publish *Pickwick Papers* and Emily Brontë was not to publish *Wuthering Heights* for a decade, we have some idea of the originality of Disraeli's achievements. Mrs Cadurcis cannot control her erratic behaviour; she provokes Cadurcis into the fatal rebellion that ultimately causes her death when she orders his fire to be put out so that he will be forced to be with her; she is jealous of Lady Annabel even while she knows intellectually that the latter does not in any way wish to interfere with her relation with her son. Unable to bring her contrary impulses into a coherent personality, Mrs Cadurcis's frustration finds an outlet in irrational jealousy of Lady Annabel's composure and judgment, and of the efficacious results such a temperament has on Lady Annabel's relationship with Venetia and her own son.

II

That Disraeli does try to constrain his propensity for writing disguised autobiography and for using his fiction as a means of creating an heroic mask affects every aspect of his art, including structure, narrative technique and tone. In his earlier novels, Disraeli's protagonists provided an outlet for his Promethean fantasies; the energy of those fantasies shaped the plot from within, sometimes almost as if the narrator and author were not in full control. If the plots of the earlier novels derived from the central characters' actions, emotions and moods (which were often thinly disguised versions of Disraeli's actions, emotions and moods), in these novels the plot tends at times to seem arbitrarily imposed by the author and to be extraneous to the characters' actions. Events that are neither determined nor controlled by force of character play a more prominent role than in Disraeli's earlier fiction. The elaborately contrived plot of the middle novels would have been at odds with one central premise of the earlier ones: that a strong character and a dynamic personality are values in themselves. In *Henrietta Temple* and *Venetia*, the narrator (but less frequently the author) for the most part maintains his distance and control; perhaps Disraeli's choice of female title characters was in part an effort to separate his inner life from the text. But despite the titles, Venetia and Henrietta Temple are not independent women in their own right; Venetia depends upon her quest for a father and husband to define her, and Henrietta is a kind of allegorical reward that awaits Ferdinand if he can settle his personal affairs. She has little vitality or control over her destiny. Both novels have reductive conclusions which ignore the complex issues previously raised. When Mr Temple inherits a fortune, the putative and oft postponed marriage between Ferdinand and Henrietta can take place. *Venetia* dispenses with Cadurcis and Herbert by means of the boating accident; the novel's focus suddenly shifts to Venetia's and her mother's mourning, and soon comes to rest on Venetia's marriage to Cadurcis's cousin, George.

As we shall see in the next two chapters, learning how to use increased objectivity was essential to the political trilogy where Disraeli's focus shifts from an interest in a grammar of personal motives to a vision of historical, political and economic cause and effect. In *Henrietta Temple* and *Venetia*, the central characters do mime some *aspects* of Disraeli's life but they are not larger-than-life depictions of his personal activities, as in *Vivian Grey*, or of his fantasies and imaginative life, as in *Contarini Fleming*. Although these two novels have women as the title figures, the male characters are the ones who embody Disraeli's values, experiences and goals. Yet he does not use Ferdinand or Marmion Herbert or Cadurcis to shape his identity as he had used the protagonists in his earlier novels. In the middle thirties he had begun to achieve a little of the recognition and success that he craved (although he was a long way from fulfilling his insatiable ambition). On the threshhold of election to Parliament, he knew that he needed to modify his public image as a dandy and eccentric in order to woo his constituency and to succeed once he entered the House of Commons.

In these novels, more conventional artistic control and more consistent point of view are achieved at the sacrifice of the double focus upon the teller as well as the tale that was so prominent a feature of the early novels. The influence of Byron, particularly *Don Juan* with its undisciplined and extravagant speaker and impulsive and uninhibited energy, virtually disappears (although that influence had played a much lesser role in *Contarini Fleming* and *Alroy* than in *Vivian Grey* and *The Young Duke*). In these middle novels Disraeli wanted his narrator to assume the stance of worldliness and urbanity that he now thought appropriate for tales of aristocratic manners and passions. Such a stance contrasts with the passionate excesses of Lord Cadurcis, Marmion Herbert and Ferdinand Armine, and of course implicitly comments on their extravagant behaviour until each of these characters is modified by experience to conform to the narrator's values. On occasion, Disraeli's former propensity to present himself in his novels as a dramatised personality and performer overwhelms the ironic detachment that he sought. In the 1853 edition of *Henrietta Temple* Disraeli slightly restrains this propensity by omitting a few passages in which the narrator dramatises himself. But the original edition of *Henrietta Temple* clearly shows more balance and maturity than his earlier novels.[6] Disraeli successfully creates a sympathetic but controlled speaker who plays a role akin to Fielding's narrator-host in *Tom Jones*; the speaker refers to Ferdinand, Henrietta and Mr Temple as they walk in the park of Armine as 'our party', and later when Ferdinand visits the Temples, he refers to them as 'our friends' (II, v, p. 88; II, vi, p. 101). Or, recalling for us the good-natured hospitality of Fielding's host, he entitles a chapter in which Ferdinand's and Henrietta's love continues to develop rapidly, 'Which I hope May Prove as Agreeable to the Reader as to Our Hero' (II, ix, p. 110). But at times the speaker abruptly shifts to a more subjective vein as when he concludes a glorious evening with a response that might have been voiced by either lover rather than the voice, 'Oh! why did this night ever have an end!' (II, x, p. 121).

Venetia shows even more consistent control of tone and voice. The following passage in *Venetia* begins as if the speaker were the performer who often intrudes into the original versions of *The Young Duke* and *Vivian Grey*, but soon the voice becomes a conventional omniscient narrator who sympathises with Lord Cadurcis, both as a unique individual and as an abstract victim:

> It has been well observed, that no spectacle is so ridiculous as the British public in one of its periodical fits of morality. . . . We must teach libertines that the English people appreciate the importance of domestic ties. Accordingly, some unfortunate man, in no respect more depraved than hundreds whose offenses have been treated with lenity, is singled out as an expiatory sacrifice. . . . He is, in truth, a sort of whipping boy, by whose vicarious agonies all the other transgressors of the same class are, it is supposed, sufficiently chastised. (IV, xvii, p. 320)

As surely as an eighteenth-century satirist, Disraeli uses his narrator to uphold the standards of civilisation. His logical, restrained and balanced prose comments on the folly of singling out a chosen victim and implicitly compares such a practice to primitive sacrificial rites.

In the mid-1830s Disraeli moved from rewriting Byron in prose to more traditional concepts of prose fiction. Disraeli was influenced by the eighteenth-century novel with its uneasy balance between romance and realism, between comedy and tragedy, between seriousness and burlesque, between satire and sentimentalism. What Leslie Stephen has called Disraeli's 'ambiguous hovering between two meanings. . . . the ironical and the serious' derives from this mixed mode of romance and realism, but in these middle novels, unlike the earlier ones, Disraeli is usually in deft control of his genre mix and his tone.[7] Recent criticism of the Victorian novel has accustomed us to different *kinds* of mimesis within the same novels. Disraeli's technique depends upon his perceptions that in life and in fiction, fantasy and realism not only exist side by side, but are sometimes incongruously superimposed upon one another like a double-exposure negative.

Disraeli deliberately evokes Richardson's tragedy *Clarissa* to raise the possibility that Ferdinand is capable of duplicity and immoral conduct. Henrietta is betrayed by a man who, as soon as he declares his love for her, appears to be something of a rake. For when Henrietta discovers that Ferdinand is betrothed to another, the subsequent shock to both her and her father culminates in his denunciation of Ferdinand as 'unworthy' of his daughter. The epistolary section, in which Henrietta becomes more desperate for his return and, finally, even for promises of his affection, inevitably suggests the form and content of Richardson's novel. The reader shares Henrietta's fears of betrayal and desertion, when, following his reply to her first letter, she apparently writes seventeen letters without receiving a response. (In his role of editor, Disraeli omits letters thirteen to seventeen in IV, ii.) Her cry at the close of the final letter teases the reader into expecting the worst: 'All my happy life I have never had a secret from my father; and now I am involved in a private engagement and a clandestine correspondence' (IV, ii, p. 212). While Henrietta is not really threatened with rape, Disraeli has cleverly raised the rhetorical stakes to the point where, by the end of the series of letters, the reader is prepared to consider the merest peccadillo on the part of Ferdinand as the ultimate outrage. Part of the reason is that Ferdinand had seemed so sensitive and delicate, if not over-sentimental, when he engaged in frequent weeping before they parted. Both Ferdinand's and Henrietta's exaggerated emotions and rapid oscillations from one emotion to another seem to owe something to the Gothic tradition as well as the sentimentalism of Richardson, Sterne, Smollett, and especially Mackenzie. Indeed, what seems to redeem Ferdinand for Disraeli is that, whatever else, he is always a man of feeling. However, in the 1853 edition, Disraeli somewhat subdued a few of Henrietta's gushier moments. If in *Henrietta Temple* he wishes at times to create the tragic density of *Clarissa*, in *Venetia* he uses the model of the eighteenth-century comic novel to lighten the novel's texture by inter-weaving humorous characters and farcical scenes into his melodramatic plot. Mrs Pauncefort (a play on Pounce-for-it, an apt name for her verbally aggressive and opportunistic personality) would not be out of place in a Fielding novel, and the incompetent magistrate Squire Mountmeadow clearly derives from the good-natured but biting social satire of Smollett. The idyll of Book VI, after the lovers are reunited, belongs to the pastoral vision of a Golden Age.

Venetia also owes some of its more intense moments to earlier forms of fiction. The sentimental scenes in which lovers dissolve in tears owe much to eighteenth-century sentimentalism. Lady Annabel's hermetic retreat, and the Herbert family secret enclosed in a locked room, derive from the mysterious, bizarre world of Gothic novels. But the illness of Henrietta and the complex portraits of the private emotions and the inner lives of Venetia, her mother and Cadurcis, belong to the world of nineteenth-century realism. At times the mixture of realism and romance works brilliantly. For example, when Cadurcis's mother's eccentricity and instability are revealed as madness within the fairy-tale world that Lady Annabel has created, the reader feels the ironic tension that implies both the impossibility and desirability of romance. Or, Plantagenet Cadurcis retreats to the world of comic romance – complete with gypsies and the stereotype cartoon figure, Squire Mountmeadow – which points up the claustrophobic and repressed nature of the world in which Plantagenet has been raised.

The two crucial biographical sources for *Henrietta Temple* are Disraeli's debts and his relationship with Henrietta Sykes. While Ferdinand Armine embodies crucial aspects of Disraeli's experience, he is not simply another of Disraeli's masks. Like Ferdinand, Disraeli was hounded by debts. In fact, Disraeli was deeply in debt throughout his life. As late as 1857, he was faced with one member of the Bentinck family calling in a large loan that he had never expected to have to repay. Jerman's study makes clear how these debts came to dominate his life and how at times 'visions of sponging houses haunted Disraeli.'[8] Disraeli knew how financial difficulty could weave itself into the very texture of a person's psyche and dominate his every thought. Despite his impetuous nature, Ferdinand has a very strong sense of family, and wants to redeem the family's financial situation and relieve his parents' anxiety. Yet, on the other hand, he is a man of passion like his grandfather and cannot, in contrast to Montfort, let his libido *follow* his self-interest. Disraeli might have perceived his own love for Henrietta Sykes in the terms Glastonbury uses to describe Ferdinand's love: 'Ferdinand is the most impetuous of human beings. His passions are a whirlwind; his volition more violent than becomes a suffering mortal' (V, ix, p. 346).

Disraeli wrote all but Books I and II of *Henrietta* after his final break with Henrietta. Interestingly, in September of 1833, the year he published *Alroy* and *Iskander*, and after he had begun *Henrietta Temple* in the full flush of his passion, he remarked on the effects of love – and he undoubtedly had Henrietta in mind – on his 'awful ambition and fiery passions'.[9] It may be that the reliance upon friends and family to complete Ferdinand's happiness reflects Disraeli's awareness that passionate love can be no more than part of one's existence. In the books of *Henrietta Temple* written in 1836, Disraeli is quite ambivalent about the 'all for love' implications of the relationship between Henrietta and Ferdinand which causes them to abandon their personal and family responsibilities. When Ferdinand turns from his commitment to Katherine, the novel displays him in an attractive light. *Henrietta Temple* celebrates both passionate love and rational merger between two complementary temperaments. If Henrietta's ardour for Ferdinand begins by celebrating the 'all for love' philosophy that dominated Disraeli's dalliance with Henrietta Sykes, the final marriage between Katherine and Montfort anticipates his practical and economically intelligent marriage to Mary Anne Lewis, an older widow who adored him and always placed his interest first.[10] Even the complications that Ferdinand must overcome before marriage to Henrietta reflect Disraeli's maturing vision of sexual love and his understanding that passion is not enough for a lasting adult relationship.

Ferdinand's erratic oscillation between guilt and self-righteousness may indicate Disraeli's state of mind towards his own adulterous relationship. In the following soliloquy, Disraeli's ironic stance seems to dissolve and be replaced by complete empathy, even though Ferdinand is manifestly unjust to Henrietta:

> When he recollected how he had loved this woman, what he had sacrificed for her, and what misery he had in consequence entailed upon himself and all those dear to him; when he contrasted his present perilous situation with her triumphant prosperity, and remembered that while he had devoted himself to love which proved false, she who had deserted him was, by a caprice of fortune, absolutely rewarded for her fickleness; he was enraged, he was disgusted, he despised himself for having been her slave; he

began even to hate her. Terrible moment when we first dare to view with feelings of repugnance the being that our soul has long idolised! It is the most awful of revelations. We start back in horror, as if in the act of profanation. (V, x, p. 349)

In the above passage, Disraeli's rendering of the way that Ferdinand's intensifying resentment gives way to self-pity and self-consuming wrath, shows how his sentences can reveal the human psyche. The shift to the first person gains its validity from our having participated in the thoughts of Ferdinand. Disraeli's use of the first-person plural to generalise Ferdinand's response is especially revealing if we recall the finality of an entry in his diary: 'Autumn 1836 – Parted forever from Henrietta'.[11] While his empathy with Ferdinand's passionate resentment occasionally disrupts his efforts to maintain distance, the novel is the livelier for it. As has been pointed out, Armine is a version of Amin, Henrietta Syke's pet name for Disraeli.[12]

Ferdinand's resilience echoes that of Disraeli, who was increasingly able to put behind him melancholy, disappointment and humiliation. Dramatising Ferdinand's regaining of his reputation may have been a psychological necessity for Disraeli whose reputation for, as Blake puts it, 'cynicism, double-dealing, recklessness and insincerity' haunted him throughout the thirties.[13] More than Disraeli's prior protagonists, Ferdinand has the ability to dispel gloom and despair no matter how severe the circumstances. No sooner had he despaired of his engagement and the family debts, than his imagination retrieves him from gloom:

Could sorrow ever enter [Ducie, the Temple home]? Was it possible that these bright halls and odorous bowers could be polluted by the miserable considerations that reigned too often supreme in his unhappy breast? An enchanted scene had suddenly risen from the earth for his delight and fascination. . . . All the troubles of the world were folly here; this was fairy-land, and he some knight who had fallen from a gloomy globe upon some starry region flashing with perennial lustre. (II, x, p. 119)

But Disraeli reveals the essence of Ferdinand's perpetual adolescence and shows how Ferdinand displaces actual circumstances with fantasies of a blissful future. For Ferdinand, as for Contarini, dreams are just as real as waking life. In a memorable dream, occuring immediately after he has met Henrietta, Katherine displaces Henrietta as he is about to pluck a flower, and the flowers are replaced by an altar from which fire shoots. Undoubtedly, such a dream reflects Ferdinand's conscience which recoils at his disloyalty towards, and putative betrayal of, Katherine. Ferdinand can temporarily exclude reality and live in the world of his own imagination, as when he becomes engaged to Henrietta. Yet in assertive, balanced, self-contained, independent clauses, Disraeli ironically mimes Ferdinand's egoism and mocks his self-inflated solipsism:

> He loved Henrietta Temple. She should be his. Who could prevent him: Was he not an Armine? Was he not the near descendant of that bold man who passed his whole life in the voluptuous indulgence of unrestrained volition! . . . He was born to follow his own pleasure; it was supreme; it was absolute; he was a despot; he set everything and everybody at defiance; and, filling a huge tumbler to the health of the great Sir Ferdinand, he retired, glorious as an emperor. (II, xiii, p. 131)

Lord Montfort and Ferdinand represent two facets of Disraeli in the mid-1830s. Disraeli knew that before he could play a political role, the impetuous, extravagant part of his character would have to be constrained, if only for appearances. Ferdinand is at times like the passionate and impulsive young man who created the early novels and involved himself in risky publishing and financial ventures. Lord Montfort is the shrewd, controlled, rational man that Disraeli knew he had to become to fulfil his ambition:

> Lord Montfort was a man of deep emotions, and of a very fastidious taste. He was a man of as romantic a temperament as Ferdinand Armine; but with Lord Montfort, life was the romance of reason; with Ferdinand, the romance of imagination. He observed finely, he calculated nicely, and his result was generally happiness. Ferdinand, on the contrary, neither observed nor calculated. His imagination created fantasies, and his impetuous passions struggled to realize them. (V, vi, p. 297)

The novel's ending is a significant indication of the direction of Disraeli's fiction. The marriages are not only important for the private lives of the four major figures, but, at least in Ferdinand's case, they prepare him for a public life in the House of Commons. Private bliss is interrelated with the fulfilment of public responsibilities; Ferdinand's character has been honed for larger responsibilities. The reformation of Ferdinand's character may be Disraeli's way of assuring his audience – and, possibly, himself – that he has overcome a profligate past and can be depended upon. That the outsiders, the Catholics, are now permitted to play a prominent role in the realm may for Disraeli be a means of illustrating to his audience the folly of excluding anyone for racial and religious reasons. It is clear that the calm, judicious Lord Montfort and the polished, tactful Mr Temple (who, however, is capable of selfish and even boorish conduct when his domination of his daughter is challenged) could not be more able men; yet they had been excluded from Parliament merely because they were Catholics.

Although written under the pressure of financial crises for the purpose of alleviating Disraeli's debts, *Henrietta Temple* shows a new sophistication in his management of point of view. Blake may overstate the change that ensues after the first two books written in 1833, when he remarks, 'From a story of passionate romance, the novel has become an urbane comedy of manners'.[14] But the novel is the better for its sophisticated awareness of the complexities of heterosexual relationships. Disraeli perceives that both Henrietta and Ferdinand are hampered in their psychosexual development by strong parental ties. Ferdinand feels guilty about his debts, but he is also resentful that his family have dissipated their estate. On one hand, he feels he deserves to marry whomever he pleases, but, on the other, he is not oblivious to his responsibilities to his family and Katherine. In this novel, Disraeli is more objective and presents a more balanced perspective that takes account of the complexities of human character. To be sure, Books One and Two of *Henrietta Temple* certainly present a simplified view of the characters; but Monypenny's complaint that in the later books the images of Ferdinand and Henrietta are both in some degree defaced ignores one of Disraeli's merits, namely, his determination to show that characters are fundamentally changed by the people they meet, the environment in which they live, and the experiences to which they are exposed.[15] It is an indication of Disraeli's maturation as an artist that he enables the reader to take a complex view of his characters. *Henrietta Temple* is satisfying in part because we cannot be comfortable with a pat judgment of either major character. Disraeli realises that circumstances define an action and what looks like heinous conduct from one perspective may be excused by subsequent revelation of extenuating circumstances. Far more than in the early novels, his presentation of characters is dynamic and evolving so that the reader is not permitted to have a set image of a complex character.

The subtlety of *Henrietta Temple* derives from Disraeli's evolving tone towards his imaginative hero. He shows how difficult it is for his hero to grow beyond emotional self-indulgence and to look at himself objectively. By moving at crucial points back and forth between the perspective of the protagonist and that of the heroine, he illustrates the validity of both characters' views of the broken engagement. In Book IV, chapter viii, he brilliantly restores our confidence in Ferdinand after several chapters in which he has been depicted unfavourably – because the narrator was rendering Henrietta's gradual discovery that she has been duped. In a sense, Disraeli has tested not only the heroine but the reader. Because Glastonbury notices that Ferdinand is ill, the reader suspends his moral judgment. Ferdinand's illness wins our sympathy as we realise that even if he is imprudent, he is not insincere. Even before that, his affirmation of his love for Henrietta and his confession of his debts make him a far more sympathetic character than would have seemed possible at the time Henrietta learned of the behaviour of Captain Armine at Bath and of his forthcoming marriage to Katherine.

III

Excepting the political trilogy, students of English literature tend to think of Disraeli's work, when they think of it at all, as that of an extravagant performer, a kind of Emperor of Ice Cream. But in truth he deserves to stand in the company of Dickens as a psychologist of children, adolescents and young adults, particularly members of these groups who are caught in emotionally claustrophobic circumstances. Since the search for a missing father is always lurking in the shadows of Disraeli's early novels, and becomes even more dominant in *Henrietta Temple*, it is hardly surprising that in *Venetia* the search for the missing parent should become the central element of the dramatic plot. The focus on fathers and children (surrogate and real) may derive from Disraeli's desire to acknowledge his father's significance to him. It may not be too much to see both Cadurcis's intellectual recognition of Marmion's worth and Venetia's emotional reconciliation with her father as indications of Disraeli's own increasing appreciation of his father. Venetia's search for her father shapes her entire life; had she not lacked a father, she would not have made the following bizarre statement to Cadurcis: 'I cannot love you as a husband should be loved. I can never love you as I love my father' (III, vii, p. 200). Despite the incestuous overtones of this statement, she is in love with an idealised and spiritualised image that she has invented. Disraeli understands how the lack of one parent and the dominance of the other can seriously distort the personality. Lady Annabel's proud self-control and desire to dominate her daughter Venetia derive from the disruption of her marriage. She has two unconscious and quite contradictory goals: to regain her husband and to revenge herself on him by destroying every trace of his paternity within their daughter.

Disraeli is never a more acute psychologist than when he writes about the loss of one or both parents. (It may be that Dickens knew *Venetia* and the title character's obsessive search for her father when he wrote of Esther Summerson's quest for her mother.) Venetia's recurrent illness is a response to being deprived of her father. She suffers physically and psychologically from not having known her father. Yet her mother's severely formal manner causes her to repress her curiosity about her father, and that repression is related to her recurring illness. Lady Annabel's attitude makes her feel that her need for a father is a betrayal of her mother. Disraeli's rendering of Venetia's inner confusion is deft. Because he does not use the psychological jargon to which we are accustomed, we may underestimate the subtlety with which he renders Venetia's self-indictment for the emotional disharmony that she feels beneath the surface of the home she shares with her mother: '[Venetia] sat mute and motionless . . . as if she were conscious of having committed some act of shame, as if she had been detected in some base and degrading deed' (II, ii, p. 110). Those who fault Disraeli for stylistic extravagance are not familiar with passages such as the one above where precise, lean phrasing conveys Venetia's inarticulate sense of moral disgrace. Disraeli's delicate artistry reveals how Venetia awakens to mystery and guilt. In a careful linear progression, the following sentence rises to a controlled climax that mimes her movement from emotional equilibrium to a conviction of her unworthiness: 'as she grew older, [she] could not refrain at times from yielding to the irresistible belief that her existence was enveloped in some mystery. Mystery too often presupposes guilt. Guilt! Who was guilty?' (II, i, p. 107). Like Esther, misery envelops her very existence, but, unlike Dickens's heroine, she does not find an emotional outlet in compensating ties or in the routine of work and responsibility. Her uncertainty and dubiety are all the more excruciating because of the perpetual presence of her proud, self-controlled, and unyielding mother.

Isolated from normal social development, Venetia tends to worship her mother. The narrator's gentle but shrewd irony depicts Venetia's idolatry of her mother, who represents to her not only a paradigm, but an apotheosis of Goodness:

> Yet while Venetia loved her mother, she could not but also respect and revere the superior being whose knowledge was her guide on all subjects, and whose various accomplishments deprived her secluded education of all its disadvantages; and when she felt that one so gifted had devoted her life to the benefit of her child, and that this beautiful and peerless lady had no other ambition but to be her guardian and attendant spirit; gratitude, fervent and profound, mingled with admiring reverence and passionate affection, and together formed a spell that encircled the mind of Venetia with talismanic sway. (II, iii, pp. 116–17)

The prose depicts the way that her mother has temporarily succeeded in creating an emotional island from which shame and guilt are banished. The problem is that as Venetia matures, she wants to be an archipelago and reach out to the world. And despite her apparent self-sufficiency, her mother also regrets her isolation. When Lady Annabel is restored to Marmion, she seems completely dominated by his intellect and personality. Like her mother, Venetia turns to God as an alternative to her emotional frustration. Later, after Dr Masham warns her that she would jeopardise her mother's health, if not her life, were she to mention her father to her, Venetia becomes obsessed with reuniting her parents because that would absolve her of the nameless guilt she feels. Her recurring illness appears whenever she feels a sense of unworthiness and incompleteness. As a fiction, her father not only plays the same role as God the Father plays for her mother, but becomes for her interchangeable with Him.

Venetia longs for the kind of marriage that eludes her mother and, perhaps unconsciously, a triumph over the mother who has deprived her of a father. Surely, Venetia's stipulation that her husband *must* be a great man – a mirror of Disraeli's compulsion that he be a great man – derives from her father's being absent and being replaced by a mythical figure that seems to her to have a larger than life stature.

Venetia feels that if she were to marry a great poet, she would offer sufficient attraction to keep him. One reason for Lady Annabel's fervent objections to Cadurcis is her unconscious fear (perhaps not unmixed with unconscious envy) lest her daughter be correct. Yet her conscious motives are her daughter's interest and her fear that her daughter's future will replicate her past.

Lady Annabel has an obsession that Cadurcis will desert her daughter as Herbert has deserted her. Subscribing to conventions and accepted social standards, she stands for a tradition of aristocratic manners and mores that is the polar opposite of Cadurcis and Herbert. As one whose life has been based on self-restraint and self-sacrifice, she regards Cadurcis's behaviour as a personal defiance of her standards which she as a surrogate mother taught him: 'And what is he now? The most lawless of the wild; casting to the winds every salutary principle of restraint and social discipline, and glorying only in the abandoned energy of self' (IV, xiv, p. 297). She is certain that were Venetia to marry Cadurcis, he would treat her daughter in the same way that Marmion did herself. Because she has failed to control Herbert or Cadurcis, whom she once regarded as a surrogate son, she is all the more determined to control her daughter's conduct. Lady Annabel makes the case against the man of imagination when she equates imagination with emotional self-indulgence. Speaking of Cadurcis, but with Herbert in mind, she says: 'Spirits like him are heartless. It is another impulse that sways their existence. It is imagination; it is vanity; it is self, disguised with glittering qualities that dazzle our weak senses, but selfishness, the most entire, the most concentrated' (IV, xiv, p. 296).

But Book VI undermines her effort to equate imagination with heartlessness. Imagination rescues the family from unhappiness. Indeed, had Herbert not been imaginative in pursuing his wife and daughter, had he not at the risk of his life zealously pursued them to Italy, and engaged the holy man to present his letter, Herbert and Lady Annabel, and the younger couple, Cadurcis and Venetia, would not have had their period of bliss. Herbert has been sufficiently modified by his experience to fulfil the role of ideal father and son. He has made the transformation, to use the terms proposed in *Henrietta Temple*, from a romantic of the imagination, to a romantic of reason. Cadurcis now seems no less suitable than Herbert for family life. Disraeli may have been proving to himself as well as to others that one who had a reputation as a dandy and an eccentric, one who had been involved in an adulterous relationship as he had with Henrietta Sykes, need not be disqualified from fulfilling the roles of father and parent.

In the guise of his fictional counterparts, Herbert and Cadurcis, Disraeli presents both Shelley and Byron as sympathetic figures and extenuates their unconventional conduct. Of course, by giving them other names, Disraeli could have it both ways; Herbert and Cadurcis do not parallel Shelley and Byron, except in the broad outlines of their careers.[16] While it adds a dimension to the novel, it is doubtful whether a modern reader requires the identification to find the novel interesting. While Herbert is nominally Shelley after he finally emerges late in the novel, his energies are rather reduced. He becomes both the typical Disraeli wisdom figure and the surrogate father who fulfils the emotional needs of Cadurcis. Cadurcis may be based on Byron, but he is also a recognisable successor to the tempestuous, impulsive, passionate hero of the prior novels, the man whose energies are never fully controlled and threaten to undermine their possessor; I am thinking of Contarini, Alroy, Vivian Grey, and even Ferdinand. Shelley and Byron provide Disraeli with models of the rebellious over-reacher to whom he was attracted, without exposing him to possible criticism for creating dissatisfied social misfits. They do so at a time when he was gaining increasing political recognition and when he knew that he was close finally to gaining the seat in Parliament that he had so frequently sought.[17] These poets dramatise the direction that he was turning his back upon. Herbert and Cadurcis are the literary and imaginative *ubermenschen* of his imagination. Their lives are ways that Disraeli tests the premise articulated by Annabel's sister-in-law: 'Everything is allowed, you know, to a genius!' (IV, vii, p. 248).

Disraeli's heroes are often forced by circumstances to retirement and travel. Retreat and exile were anathemas to Disraeli the political figure, but they represented an attractive alternative to the private man haunted by debts. While providing a necessary outlet for Disraeli from frustrated ambition, the travelogue which occurs in virtually every one of Disraeli's first six novels is at times barely related to the action. (Even the young Duke travels about England, stopping at various castles.) Undoubtedly one reason that Disraeli took his protagonist on tour was to extend the length of the novels to three, full, separately issued volumes. But dramatising memories of his past travels, travels undertaken to relieve disappointment and ill health, was restorative for himself as well as the characters he created. The pastoral scenes in the Apennines are typical of Disraeli's use of place to create a state of mind.

Both the younger Herbert and Lord Cadurcis, prior to meeting Herbert, represent the self that Disraeli, rather reluctantly but quite consciously, is in the process of putting behind him, while the mature Herbert represents the idealised philosophic, mature man that Disraeli is trying to become. After the most tumultuous, unconventional life, Herbert discovers that human happiness resides in family ties. The dialogue between Disraeli's two surrogates, Cadurcis and Herbert, is really a dialogue between two aspects of himself. Cadurcis's iconoclastic view, that 'men have always been fools and slaves, and fools and slaves they always will be' (VI, iv, 415), parallels one strand of Disraeli's own thinking. Yet, like his character, Disraeli had experienced the erratic fluctuation of public opinion and knew what it was to be in public disfavour (for example, when *Vivian Grey* was ridiculed and lampooned). Herbert, the man who carried individualism to an extreme, renounces his Byronic quest and speaks for Disraeli's commitment to community values: 'Love . . . is an universal thirst for a communion, not merely of the senses, but of our whole nature, intellectual, imaginative and sensitive. He who finds his antitype, enjoys a love perfect and enduring; time cannot change it, distance cannot remove it; the sympathy is complete' (VI, vi, p. 429).

Disraeli wrote of the modification and maturation of two men of genius when he wished to convince both an electorate that kept rejecting him, and those party leaders who selected candidates for Parliament, of his suitability for office. He wanted his readers to identify him with prophetic figures such as Shelley and Byron but also he wanted to show them that these figures could mature and embrace socially acceptable philosophic views. The novel gradually establishes the authority of Herbert and discards Cadurcis's cynicism. Herbert is the philosopher of a kind of optimistic upward evolution with which his fellow Tories could feel comfortable. That both Cadurcis and his cousin George fulfil their public responsibilities in Parliament, while Herbert has helped lead a revolution, shows that Disraeli retains an interest in the public world even when writing about family relationships.

Herbert's theoretical optimism reflects the utopian and prophetic strand in Disraeli's thinking which places him as well as his character within the Visionary Company of which we spoke in the last chapter. While Disraeli rejected utilitarianism and the mid-nineteenth-century faith in progress and the perfectibility of man, he believed the most profound questions might be answered by the mind of man. Herbert's utopian ideal that 'the principle of life' may be discovered and that man may attain earthly immortality anticipates the search for spiritual truth in *Tancred*: 'The annihilation of death . . . will . . . be produced by some vast and silent and continuous operation of nature, gradually effecting some profound and comprehensive alteration in her order' (VI, iv, pp. 416–17).

The ambitiousness of Herbert's vision, if not its profundity, testifies to the kind of cosmic and prophetic view to which Disraeli aspired in the 1830s. If the younger and unseen Herbert is Shelley, the rebel and iconoclast, the mature Herbert gives us an insight into the visionary and imaginative pretensions of Disraeli's mind at this time. Like the descent of the angel in *Tancred*, the actual details are unimportant as predictions, but illustrative of the kind of fantasy that Disraeli could articulate and temporarily believe. Yet, as Blake writes, Disraeli was 'one of those actors who enter so deeply into their role that for the time being they suspend disbelief and really live the part which they enact.'[18]

Disraeli's father had inquired after learning that he was writing *Henrietta Temple*: 'How . . . will the fictionist assort with the politician? Most deeply am I regretting that you will find it necessary to return to drink of the old waters'.[19] *Venetia* is in part a response to that inquiry. It is extremely significant that Disraeli has the mature Marmion Herbert quote Shelley's famous statement that 'poets are the unacknowledged legislators of the world' (VI, viii, p. 438). Self-conscious about his failure to make any mark as a poet, after the first three books of *The Revolutionary Epick* (1834) had been unenthusiastically received, Disraeli wished to establish the legitimacy of his novels. His original preface to *Alroy* in 1832, which boasted of an innovative merging of prose and poetry based on the use of rhyme and rhythm in his romance, reflected his desire that he be taken seriously as an artist, even though he was writing in prose.[20] Disraeli evokes Shelley's words to convince both his father and himself of the importance of his creative endeavours. When Herbert says of Cervantes's work, '[Cervantes] is the same to this age as if he had absolutely wandered over the plains of Castile and watched in the Sierra Morena', he is applying Shelley's words that only a poem is 'universal, and contains within itself the germ of a relation to whatever motives or actions have place in the possible varieties of human nature' (IV, i, p. 394).[21] Through his character, Disraeli is claiming the same position for prose as Shelley did for poetry.[22] When Herbert quotes Shelley, Disraeli the novelist includes himself in the vast claims for imaginative literature implied by the invocation of Shelley's spirit. Nor is it accidental that Herbert is moved, not by a poet's, but by a novelist's vision of the golden age. It is Disraeli's position that the *imaginative writer*, not merely the poet, combines the roles of legislator and prophet.[23]

3 Progressive Dubiety: The Discontinuity of Disraeli's Political Trilogy

I

A brief look at *Popanilla* (1828), Disraeli's early imaginary voyage, is an appropriate prelude to our discussion of the trilogy. *Popanilla* is undoubtedly indebted to Swift's *Gulliver's Travels* and *The Tale of a Tub* and probably also to Johnson's *Rasselas* and Voltaire's *Candide* and *Zadig*, and could be discussed in terms of those predecessors. But I begin this chapter with *Popanilla* because Disraeli discovered in that work that he could use fiction to express his political and philosophic views. In his first example of political fiction, he avoided character analysis and a coherent unified plot, and relied upon loosely related and implausible episodes and one-dimensional caricatures in the service of ideas. His insistence on subordinating his imagination to his ideas prepared him for writing the Young England trilogy – *Coningsby* (1844), *Sybil* (1845) and *Tancred* (1847) – in which ideas and principles are paramount. But in those novels, as we shall see, there is ample room for character exploration and for Disraeli's increasingly sophisticated narrative technique.

In *Popanilla*, Disraeli voices his suspicion of all systems and dogma and mocks the exclusive reliance on reason as much as any particular system. *Popanilla* begins by satirising utilitarianism, but soon moves on to satirise many of the fundamental assumptions on which early nineteenth-century British economic and political life were based. The title character Popanilla lives contentedly on the Isle of Fantasie until he discovers knowledge in the form of books that are washed ashore after a shipwreck. Fantasie is described as 'another Eden' where summer is perpetual and where the people 'are an innocent and a happy, though a voluptuous and ignorant race' (i, p. 367). Popanilla enjoys an idyllic existence until he immerses himself in books about

'Useful Knowledge'. His education makes him dissatisfied with his lot; he discovers that 'he and his fellow-islanders were nothing more than a horde of useless savages' (iv, p. 374).

Disraeli's ironic point is that prior to discovering the books of 'Useful Knowledge', Popanilla seemed to be in a Paradise, but man's zeal to improve himself is his curse: 'In answer to those who affect to admire that deficient system of existence which they style simplicity of manners, and who are perpetually committing the blunder of supposing that every advance towards perfection only withdraws man further from his primitive and proper condition, Popanilla triumphantly demonstrated that no such order as that which they associated with the phrase "state of nature" ever existed' (iv, p. 378). Paradoxically, this self-awareness of his misery makes him superior to his fellows. He digests the principles of utility; his lecture to the king in which he contends that man is 'a developing animal' is a parody of utilitarianism: 'The life of man was therefore to be passed in a moral and material development until he had consummated his perfection' (iv, p. 377).

After Popanilla becomes a nuisance, the king sends him in search of new territories. Popanilla discovers Vraibleusia – Disraeli's ironic version of England. A 'developing animal himself', Popanilla progresses from anonymous citizen to captain to ambassador to Plenipotentiary and Prince. His stature derives not from accomplishments or abilities of his own, but from the commercial hopes that he arouses upon his arrival as a stranger in Vraibleusia. When the Vraibleusian king's fleet returns without having opened trade with Fantasia, or even *finding* Popanilla's home, Popanilla's position is reduced to one of the anonymously unemployed. Disraeli is satirising a materialistic culture that values a person according to the commercial gain it can reap from him.

Sexual licence seems to be a major characteristic of the utopia Disraeli imagines on the Isle of Fantasie. No mention is made of families or children, and the one kind of knowledge with which the people are blessed is that of 'the art of making love' (i, p. 367). Each evening they retire in pairs after the evening frolic. Fantasie is an adolescent male fantasy. Popanilla originally seeks knowledge to compensate for sexual disappointment.[1] 'Dance' becomes virtually a euphemism for intercourse throughout the first chapters. Knowledge of utility, Disraeli implies, stifles sexuality and emasculates instinctive vitality. Popanilla's potential converts are saved from following him by 'the embraces of their former partners, and their utilitarianism dissolved in the arms of those they once so rudely rejected' (V, p. 385). Perhaps one reason why the Vraibleusian fleet cannot locate Fantasie is that it represents an illicit sexual fantasy. It is almost as if Disraeli's psyche in 1828 cannot sanction the fusion of the English code of behaviour with his own libidinous, and often licentious, fantasies.

Popanilla has journeyed from a literal world, where the names of things signify things, to a more complex world where metaphors and allegory are possible and where the name of things may signify values and ideas. Disraeli's brilliant handling of the extended metaphor which equates appetite for fruit with spiritual needs foreshadows his organisation of narrative incidents in the trilogy into historically significant patterns. The chapter on fruits is nothing less than a summary of English ecclesiastical history. Appropriately, Catholics eat pineapples (a fruit chosen because its thorniness suggests Christ's thorns), the Puritans eat crab apples (chosen because of the Puritans' supposedly dour and gloomy disposition), and the Anglicans eat pineapples derived from suckers rather than from the original plant. Describing Henry VIII's expropriation of church property, Disraeli writes: 'In spite of the wishes of the majority of the nation, the whole of the dealers were one day expelled from the island, and the Managers of the Statue immediately took possession of their establishments' (xiv, p. 442). The statue is Disraeli's ironic personification of the English monarchy, and the managers are those in whose hands the actual power rests. Men 'universally [feed] upon those delightful productions of Nature which are nourished with the dews of heaven, and which live for ever in its breath' (xiv, p. 438). The association of fruit with heaven urges the reader to perceive the connection. As soon as the stranger brings pineapples, his 'gift', those who taste the fruit 'fell upon their knees to worship him, vowing that the distributor of such delight must be more than man' (xiv, p. 439). But the stranger protested their 'adoration' and 'with an air of great humility . . . told them that, far from being superior to common mortals, he was, on the contrary, one of the lowliest of the human race. . . . merely a market-gardener on a great scale' (xiv, p. 439). Christ by tradition is the gardener of souls. Disraeli's readers would have recalled the passage in John 20:11–16 in which Jesus appears to Mary Magdalen only to have her mistake Him for the gardener. The Vraibleusians eventually forget the 'market-gardener', and confuse the servants of the gardener with the gardener himself, and mistake the Prince of the World for the real source of pineapples. That the

Prince of the World is the Pope and that the Prince of the World also traditionally implies the devil suggests Disraeli's ambivalence to Catholicism in 1828. The chapter concludes with an ironic view of 'an universal toleration of fruit' which in fact excludes those from office or service who are 'not supplied from the Government depots' (xiv, p. 449).

Lucien Wolf has remarked upon *Popanilla's* importance to Young England and the trilogy.

> Indeed, it is in the anti-Benthamism and anti-Ricardoism of *Popanilla* that we have the first glimpse of the Romanticism which afterwards inspired the 'Young England' party, and was turned into channels of practical politics by the struggle against Peel's surrender to Free Trade. There are whole pages of *Popanilla* – especially Chapter IV – which are clearly the raw material out of which was ultimately evolved the anti-Utilitarianism preached by Sidonia in *Coningsby* and by Gerard in *Sybil.*[2]

Although later Disraeli became an advocate of particular positions that he satirises in *Popanilla* such as the Corn Laws and the Colonial system, this early novella foreshadows many of Young England's values, especially its dislike of materialism and expedience. For example, *Tancred* develops *Popanilla*'s disdain for a culture that reduces man to a machine and that glorifies reason and logic at the expense of mystery and imagination.

II

As Blake has remarked, Young England was 'a sort of nostalgic escape from the disagreeable present to the agreeable but imaginary past'.[3] Young England was a movement in the early 1840s which despised utilitarianism, middle-class liberalism, and centralised government. It sought to return England to the feudal and monarchal antecedents of its national youth. While its other two leaders, George Smythe and Lord John Manners, were primarily young aristocrats, Disraeli was the central figure. Now close to forty, Disraeli for the first time had some political importance. George Smythe was a man of great gifts, but uncertain judgment, who was at least in part the model for Coningsby. Lord John Manners lacked Smythe's extraordinary potential and scintillating intellect, but was a kindly, high-principled man who epitomised the integrity and idealism of Young England. Manners was the model for Lord Henry Sidney in *Coningsby*. Alexander Baillie-Cochrane, the next most prominent figure after Disraeli, Smythe and Manners, was the model for Buckhurst in *Coningsby*. A Scotsman of Disraeli's age, Baillie-Cochrane played a lesser role but was the fourth member of the founding group. Although Disraeli wrote that he was 'the leader of a party chiefly of the youth and new members',[4] Young England was never a numerical factor, only including about a dozen at best; even Disraeli, Smythe, Manners and Baillie-Cochrane, the four central members, did not always agree on major issues.

They sought to form a party composed of the younger, more vigorous members of the Tory party, but Young England never became more than a small group of like-minded Tories who, as Disraeli put it in the 1870 General Preface to the collected edition, 'Living much together, without combination . . . acted together'.[5] Although on occasion some of Peel's supporters voted with them on certain issues, Young England never achieved a specific legislative programme. For example, Young England stood firmly for the Corn Laws, even after Peel had begun to waver. As Steven Graubard has written, 'Young England took upon itself the task of bringing the party back to a greater consciousness of his historic traditions'.[6] Typical not only of the kind of community for which Young England longed, but of the romantic nostalgia that formed the basis of their political programme, are the following lines by Manners:

> Each knew his place – king, peasant, peer, or priest –
> The greater owned connexion with the least;
> From rank to rank the generous feeling ran
> And linked society as man to man.[7]

Young England argued that the poor should be cared for by conscientious aristocrats and a responsive Church rather than administrative structures created by Poor Laws. They idealised the role of the Pre-Reformation Catholic Church in creating community ties and in fulfilling community responsibilities.

For Disraeli, Young England was a sustaining personal fiction, a political programme that provided an alternative not only to Chartism and Utilitarianism, but to the practical considerations of advancing his position. Like Disraeli's dream that a coterie of youth would revive England, *Coningsby* reflects a mixture of idealism, fantasy and escapism. But in *Sybil* Disraeli comes to grips with the economic deprivation experienced by the rural and urban poor and seems to be ambivalent about the notion that one heroic man can make a substantive difference.[8]

By the time Disraeli wrote *Tancred* in 1846, Young England had virtually disintegrated following the controversy over funding the Maynooth Seminary in late 1845. Disraeli sharply disagreed with Peel's proposal to increase the Government grant to Maynooth, whose purpose was the education of Catholic priests. Influenced by the Oxford Movement and their family ties to Ireland, Smythe and Manners supported Peel. Disraeli took the opposing position but used the debate as the occasion for a devastating attack on Peel, whom he had never forgiven for passing him over for office in 1840 and whose conduct and politics he attacked in *Coningsby* and *Sybil*.

III

Disraeli's Young England novels – *Coningsby*, or *The New Generation* (1844); *Sybil*, or *The Two Nations* (1845); and *Tancred*, or *The New Crusade* (1847) – are a radical departure from his earlier fiction. Politics were more than a vocation for Disraeli. In the 1840s, his political life seemed to fulfil for him what George Eliot speaks of as 'that idea of duty, that recognition of something to be lived for beyond the mere satisfaction of self'.[9] For the first time since he began his parliamentary career in 1837, he returned to fiction because he understood the potential of presenting his ideas in an imaginative framework.

Disraeli's General Preface, written in 1870, should be understood as a retrospective statement of intention, not as a substantive critical commentary. In that preface, he writes:

> The derivation and character of political parties; the condition of the people which had been the consequence of them; the duties of the Church as a main remedial agency in our present state; were the principal topics which I intended to treat, but I found they were too vast for the space I had allotted to myself.
>
> They were all launched in 'Coningsby' but the origin and condition of political parties, the first portion of the theme, was the only one completely handled in that work.

> Next year (1845), in SYBIL, OR THE TWO NATIONS, I considered the condition of the people. . . .
>
> In recognizing the Church as a powerful agent in the previous development of England . . . it seemed to me that the time had arrived when it became my duty to . . . consider the position of the descendants of that race who had been the founders of Christianity. Familiar as we all are now with such themes, the House of Israel being now freed from the barbarism of mediaeval misconception, and judged like other races by their contributions to the existing sum of human welfare, and the general influence of race on human action being universally recognized as the key of history, the difficulty and hazard of touching for the first time on such topics cannot now be easily appreciated. But public opinion recognized both the truth and sincerity of these views, and, with its sanction, in TANCRED OR THE NEW CRUSADE, the third portion of the Trilogy, I completed their development.

Disraeli's trilogy presents both a political geography and a historical survey of England, and simultaneously suggests how England could experience a political and moral rebirth.

If finally the Young England trilogy does not always hold together as an aesthetic entity or as a coherent polemical statement, it does have substantial aesthetic and intellectual continuities. And where it lacks continuity is not entirely a fault. As we shall see, the differences among the novels give the reader who reads them consecutively multiple perspectives on England's moral and political controversies in the period from the Reform Bill to the late 1840s. The changes in form and theme from novel to novel prevent the reader from taking a complacent one-dimensional view of complex political and religious problems. That Disraeli shifts attention from character to public issues and back to character as he moves from *Coningsby* to *Sybil* and then to *Tancred*, and that within each novel he focuses alternatively on politics and on an individual's moral life, emphasise a major theme in the trilogy, namely how the individual's life is woven into the web of the community.

Despite the 1870 Preface, we should not forget the intensely personal tone of his later letters. The following comment is quite typical: 'My books are the history of my life – I don't mean a vulgar photograph of incidents, but the psychological development of my character' (27 September 1875).[10] Like Tennyson, Carlyle, Mill and Newman, Disraeli responded with a desperate search for absolutes to a world of moral turmoil. That Disraeli's narrators and major characters speak *ex cathedra* in generalisations and abstractions may derive from his desire to emulate in the fabric of his fiction the scope and seriousness of Victorian philosophical and religious tracts. The trilogy of the 1840s is his *Apologia*. Behind the dramatisation of the education of Tancred, Coningsby and Egremont lies Disraeli's quest for the principles with which he could structure his public life. He continually asserted dogma to convince himself of its value, although as with Newman, the nature of the dogma was continually in flux. The political ideals discovered by his Young England heroes became, for a time, the tenets of his own political and moral creed.

Disraeli's motives for writing the trilogy were complex. He undoubtedly wanted to articulate political and moral principles, in part no doubt to erase the notoriety that he had acquired, owing to as Blake puts it 'the continued refusal of the *Quarterly Review* even to mention his name, the alleged tergiversations in his early political career, his rickety finances, the extravagancies of his novels . . . his mysterious half-foreign appearance, and the virulent abuse, much of which stuck, hurled at him by malignant journalists.[11] He also wanted to establish the importance of Judaism to western civilisation.[12] He created Sidonia as a mouthpiece to *argue* for the historical significance of the Jewish people in *Coningsby* and in the first two books of *Tancred*. But it is Tancred's pilgrimage to Jerusalem for 'Asian spirituality' and his discovery of the Hebraic basis of Christianity that *dramatise* Disraeli's intense personal need to reconcile his Jewish origins with the Christian religion. He believed that Christianity was completed Judaism, although he may have unconsciously taken this position because of his need to justify his own conversion. He argued in *Lord George Bentinck* (1852) that a Jew converted to Christianity professes the 'whole Jewish religion and believes in Calvary as well as Sinai.'[13] In his study of Disraeli's Jewish aspect, Cecil Roth writes:

> But it seems as though the Christianity which he professed, quite sincerely, in his own mind was not that of the established Church, but a Judaic ethical monotheism, of which the Jew Jesus was the last and greatest exponent. As he put it, Christianity was a developed Judaism and Judaism a preparation for Christianity. Jesus was the ideal scion of the Jewish people . . . in whose teachings the Mosaic faith received its culmination, the New Testament being the perfection, and climax, of the Old.[14]

Disraeli's self-confidence in part depended upon his belief that the Jews deserved esteem as an especially gifted *race*. Often, and with considerable justification, Disraeli is accused of political expedience and intellectual legerdemain. But the defence of Jews was an article of faith. Disraeli risked his chances for leadership when he insisted in 1847 that his friend Baron Lionel de Rothschild be allowed to take his seat in Parliament without taking the Parliamentary oath 'on the true faith of a Christian'.[15] On that occasion, he invoked arguments similar to those that appeared in both *Tancred* and later in *Lord George Bentinck* to support the Baron's position.

IV

Let us review the ties that bind the novels together. The trilogy's three heroes – Coningsby, Egremont and Tancred – are young scions of great families estranged from those charged with raising them. Each is expected by family circumstances and social convention to fulfil a predetermined pattern. But each of the young men gradually becomes disillusioned with his expected paradigm of development and those who counsel it, and is gradually re-educated to a new set of values. Coningsby and Egremont learn that Monmouth and Marney are models that they must not follow. Monmouth expected his grandson, Coningsby, to be a Conservative representing Monmouth, the aristocracy, and the Tory party – in that order. Egremont's family typifies the aristocratic family which ignores the interests of the common people. On the other hand, Tancred eschews the values of his parents, who are in many ways the models of a responsible aristocracy, and of the men whom the previous novels have established as the basis of a resurgent aristocracy: Coningsby, Egremont and Henry Sidney.

Coningsby, *Sybil*, and to an extent *Tancred*, share Disraeli's rather reductive response to what he felt was Whig propaganda disguised as history: 'Generally speaking, all the great events have been distorted, most of the important causes concealed, some of the principal characters never appear, and all who figure are so misunderstood and misrepresented, that the result is a complete mystification . . .' (*Sybil*, I, iii, p. 17). According to Disraeli, a 'Venetian Constitution' – by which is meant the reduction of the power of the throne by the Whig oligarchy until the King is no more than a 'doge' – has displaced the English system. For Disraeli, Charles I is a martyr, and the Glorious

Revolution is 'The Dutch Invasion of 1688' which resulted because 'the resources of Holland, however inconsiderable, were inadequate to sustain him in his internecine rivalry with the great sovereign of France' (*Sybil*, I, iii, p. 23). Those families who deposed James II in the name of civil and religious liberty were the very Whig families who formed the Venetian party and who 'in one century plundered the church to gain the property of the people and in another century changed the dynasty to gain the power of the crown' (*Sybil*, I, iii, p. 14). With the continuing decline of the monarchy and the accelerating abnegation of responsibility on the part of the aristocracy who once cared for those living on their land, the common people now had no one to champion their cause. The established Anglican Church did not provide either spiritual solace or the hospitality and charity that the Catholic Church once provided for the common people before Henry VIII seized the abbeys and monasteries. Despite its intent to show how spiritual values might be revived, *Tancred* does not examine the implications of this historiography as it informs English life. Walter Houghton has noted:

> When the Victorian period began, all the prerequisites for hero worship were present: the enthusiastic temper, the conception of the superior being, the revival of Homeric mythology and medieval ballad, the identification of great art with grand style, the popularity of Scott and Byron, and the living presence of Napoleonic soldiers and sailors. . . . Hero worship . . . exorcises the antisocial forces of personal or class ambition, bred by the doctrines of liberty and equality, and in their place calls forth the uniting emotions of loyalty and reverence for one great man who is our common leader.[16]

The trilogy explores the possibilities of heroism in an age which is epitomised for Disraeli by Vavasour, a secondary character in *Coningsby*, who 'is the quintessence of order, decency, and industry' and who complacently expresses the Benthamite creed that civilisation is 'the progressive development of the faculties of man' (*Tancred*, II, xiv, p. 146–8). Coningsby's ambition is admirable and necessary because the adult world into which he is born is corrupt and hypocritical. For Disraeli, as for Carlyle, ambition is not self-intoxication, but a noble quality that directs a man to follow in the heroic footsteps of the great men of history:[17]

> It was that noble ambition, the highest and the best, that must be born in the heart and organised in the brain, which will not let a man be content, unless his intellectual power is recognised by his race, and desires that it should contribute to their welfare. It is the heroic feeling, the feeling that in old days produced demi-gods; without which no State is safe; without which political institutions are meat without salt; the Crown is a bauble, the Church an establishment, Parliaments debating-clubs, and Civilisation itself but a fitful and transient dream. (*Coningsby*, V, i, pp. 259–60)

The 'highest' and the 'best' ambition stirs a man to strive for recognition and (*secondly*, according to the revealing syntax) to contribute to the nation. Indeed, Disraeli never quite convinces us that the fulfilment of his heroes' resplendent visions and aspirations is *not* more important than the principles on which those aspirations are nominally based and the people whom they presumably are to benefit.

Because Coningsby and Egremont are fatherless and Tancred is estranged from his parents' values, each seeks the advice of a surrogate father. With the aid of his daughter, Sybil, Gerard educates Egremont about the needs and rights of the common people. Sidonia provides Coningsby and Tancred with essential wisdom. (Retrospectively, we find some of his advice disarmingly naïve, if not unpalatable; he tells Tancred, 'All is race; there is no other truth' [*Tancred*, II, xiv, p. 149].) At a crucial point, each of Disraeli's Young England heroes is tempted to withdraw from his quest for sustaining truths. Coningsby is discouraged after he is given short shrift in Monmouth's will: 'The Great Seal indeed! It was the wild excitement of despair, the frenzied hope that blends inevitably with absolute ruin, that could alone have inspired such a hallucination! His unstrung heart deserted him. His energies could rally no more' (*Coningsby*, IX, iv, pp. 454–5). Disgusted with his brother and the superficiality of fashionable life, Egremont withdraws from his responsibilities and takes on the identity of Franklin. Tancred is not only almost dissuaded from undertaking his journey by the insipid Lady Constance and the disingenuous Lady Bertie and Bellair but, more importantly, temporarily loses faith in his purpose after reaching Jerusalem: 'Was he, then, a stranger there? Uncalled, unexpected, intrusive, unwelcome? Was it a morbid curiosity, or the proverbial restlessness of a satiated aristocrat, that had drawn him to these wilds?' (*Tancred*, IV, iv, p. 264).

In each novel of the trilogy, Disraeli's persona speaks not as a Member of Parliament, which Disraeli had been since 1837, but as an enlightened and perceptive aristocrat. One implicit premise of the trilogy is that a prophetic voice could arouse the sensibilities of his fellow aristocrats to the spiritual and economic plight of the people and to the need for restoring the Monarchy and the Church to their former dignity. Disraeli's surrogate self, the narrator, is implicitly one of those 'primordial and creative mind[s] . . . [that could] say to his fellows: Behold, God has given me thought; I have discovered truth; and you shall believe!' (*Coningsby*, II, iii, p. 109). The comprehensive political consciousness of the speaker is the intellectual and moral position toward which the hero of each volume of the trilogy finally develops. The narrator empathetically traces the quest of the potential hero (Egremont, Coningsby and Tancred) to discover the appropriate values by which he can order his own life and fulfil the prominent public role that he feels himself obliged to play. (The complete absence of irony toward the protagonist occasionally has the negative effect of neutralising Disraeli's wit and vivacity.)

According to Disraeli's intended argument, each of the protagonists overcomes dubiety and anxiety because he convinces himself that he possesses the unique intellectual and moral potential to shape not merely his own life, but the very fabric of historical process. Each protagonist's quest is conceived as an heroic quest to discover the values essential for a new breed of political leaders who will recognise the supremacy of the monarchy and the importance of serving the common people. Coningsby's ambition and self-confidence, Egremont's compassion and consciousness of the miseries of others, and Tancred's spiritual faith and willingness to act on behalf of his beliefs are the ideals to which others (and *others* for Disraeli meant his aristocratic audience and hence potential political leaders) must strive. The quest for values takes place against the background of Tadpole's and Taper's political expedience; the self-indulgence and arrogance of such aristocrats as Marney and Monmouth; the spiritual emptiness of entire communities such as Wodgate; and the recurring periods of poverty. The trilogy satirises a decadent aristocracy lacking in vitality and a sense of responsibility, and a parliamentary system that seems divorced from the people for whom it is responsible. The satire also focuses on those who, despite their pretensions, are without principles or faith: men like Rigby, Morley and Fakredeen, who betray the protagonists.

V

In many significant ways, however, the three novels are separate and distinct. In the Young England novels, Disraeli used three different genres of fiction. *Coningsby* is a *Bildungsroman* concerned with the intellectual and moral development of the potential leader. *Sybil*, heavily borrowing from Blue Book material, is a polemical novel that primarily focuses on the socio-economic conditions that need to be remedied. And *Tancred* is an imaginary voyage in the tradition of *Gulliver's Travels*, *Robinson Crusoe* and Disraeli's own neglected *Popanilla*.

Coningsby opens against the background of political turmoil that existed prior to the debate on The Reform Bill of 1832. Coningsby is the grandson of the arrogant megalomaniac Lord Monmouth, who, like Lord Steyne of *Vanity Fair*, is based upon Lord Hertford. Monmouth has undertaken to educate his orphaned grandson, although he has broken all ties with the boy's father, his youngest son, because he disapproved of his marriage. Coningsby is a young man of enormous potential; as he matures it is clear that he combines the necessary ability, ambition, intellect, judgment and imagination to become a political leader. As the novel traces his education and development, Coningsby learns from his travels through England, and gradually rejects the examples of parasites and social climbers, such as Rigby, and dissolute aristocrats, such as Prince Colonna.

As Coningsby is about to leave Eton, he is uncertain of his future, in part because he lacks both a sure economic base and family ties. He takes a roundabout journey to visit the grandfather. He meets Sidonia, a sophisticated and wise Jew of great wealth and vast learning who becomes his mentor and begins to shape Coningsby's mind toward the goal of becoming a great leader. He visits his friend Lord Henry Sidney at Beaumanoir and meets Lord Henry's father who provides an example of the benevolent aristocracy. He visits Eustace Lyle and sees how monastic customs and Catholic customs have been revived to enrich the spiritual lives and to increase the well-being of the common people. Next he visits his friend Oswald Millbank whose father is a Manchester manufacturer. He learns that a factory at its best resembles the feudal system in its hierarchical organisation, clearly defined responsibilities, and concern for the welfare of the workers. Finally Coningsby visits his family home, Coningsby Castle, where Monmouth rules without concern for his neighbours or the common people, and without the warmth and grace to be found at Beaumanoir.

Back at Eton, Coningsby and his friends form a group dedicated to a Conservatism that wishes to revive the Church and Monarchy and to restore the aristocracy's sense of responsibility. On a visit to Monmouth in Paris he meets Edith Millbank, his friend's sister. When Monmouth wants to contest his hated rival, the senior Millbank, in an election, he asks his grandson to be his candidate. But Coningsby refuses, not only because he does not want to offend the Millbank family, but also because he could not in good conscience vote with the present Conservatives. When Coningsby refuses to run, Monmouth vows to cut him off from the family as he had cut off Coningsby's father. Monmouth soon dies and leaves Coningsby a very small legacy. But at the urging of his son, the elder Millbank withdraws his candidate and allows Coningsby to run in his place. He also approves his marriage to Edith which gives Coningsby the economic base he needs, even before he inherits, as he soon does, most of Monmouth's estate upon the death of the latter's illegitimate daughter.

The effectiveness of *Coningsby* as a work of art depends upon Disraeli's establishing a relationship between the private theme – the development of Coningsby's abilities as a potential leader – and the public theme – the need for revivifying England's political institutions. The insipid political gossip and private debauchery of both the aristocracy and their myrmidons give convincing support to Millbank's call for a natural aristocracy of virtue, talent and property. As a comparative newcomer to wealth, the senior Millbank may be a bit unpolished and prone to anger, but how preferable is his integrity to the amorality and cynicism of Monmouth and his followers. Such dramatic interest as there is depends upon whether Coningsby will develop into an exceptional man, not upon whether he will become simply a moral and capable one. Sidonia, Millbank and Lyle provide significant *examples* of alternative life styles to those espoused by Monmouth and his followers. Part of the dramatic potential of *Coningsby* is lost because the rather priggish protagonist's 'tempters' hold no appeal for him. Coningsby's superego does not require the influence of Lyle, the elder Millbank, and especially Sidonia to reject the duplicity of Rigby, the solipsism of Monmouth, and the cynicism and decadence of irresponsible aristocrats, including the Colonna family.

Coningsby's growth is measured by a kind of intellectual barometer: his acceptance of the views held by Sidonia (whose views generally echo the narrator's) is the index of his development. As is often the case in a *Bildungsroman* employing an omniscient third-person narrator, Disraeli's narrator expresses the values which the protagonist comes to accept. Thus there is a gradually narrowing distance between the narrator, Disraeli's surrogate, and Coningsby, as the latter becomes a spokesman for the values of the former. Monmouth speaks for the position that places family before party, and party before nation: 'The only person to whom you are responsible is your own relation, who brings you in. . . . All you have got to do is to vote with your party' (*Coningsby*, VIII, iii, pp. 406–7). But the principled Coningsby can accept neither his grandfather's values nor support the Conservative party as it is presently constituted; and his reasons are identical with Disraeli's political views in 1844:

> I have for a long time looked upon the Conservative party as a body who have betrayed their trust; more from ignorance, I admit, than from design; yet clearly a body of individuals totally unequal to the exigencies of the epoch; and indeed unconscious of its real character. . . .
>
> What we want, sir, is not to fashion new dukes and furbish up old baronies; but to establish great principles which may maintain the realm and secure the happiness of the people. Let me see authority once more honoured; a solemn reverence again the habit of our lives; let me see property acknowledging, as in the old days of faith, that labour is his twin brother, and that the essence of all tenure is the performance of duty; let results such as these be brought about, and let me participate, however, feebly, in the great fulfilment, and public life then indeed become a noble career, and a seat in Parliament an enviable distinction. (*Coningsby*, III, iii, pp. 407, 411)

In terms of his career *Coningsby* may have been the most important novel that Disraeli wrote. He not only defined his political philosophy at a crucial time in his career, but he created in Coningsby and Sidonia two important fictional models for himself. Coningsby, the man who is elected to Parliament in his early twenties and who seems destined for leadership, enacted a fantasy that sustained Disraeli. He discovered anew his potential to be a political leader by imagining himself as Coningsby, who overcomes apparent loss of wealth and position by means of diligence, self-confidence and extraordinary ability. Never mind that this fantasy figure does not have the burden of Disraeli's past notoriety, his Jewish ancestry, and his debts, or that at the age of 40 it was no longer possible for Disraeli to achieve pre-eminence at a precocious age. Imagining that merit was acknowledged and setbacks overcome played an essential if indeterminate role in fortifying his self-confidence. As he wrote as spokesman for and leader of Young England, he embraced the romance of Coningsby's heroism; this explains *Coningsby's* oscillation between *Bildungsroman* and novel of purpose.

Coningsby is Disraeli's last effort to imagine an heroic adolescence. He clearly enjoys his fantasies about Coningsby's life at Eton. In *Coningsby*, Disraeli seems to be trying to rewrite his own past for his audience if not for himself, perhaps believing that his aspirations required that he be thought of as an Eton man. The outsider who wanted to become an insider, be becomes the spokesman for idealising the public school. He implies that the hierarchical structure among the students is a means of developing potential leaders. Moreover, the friendship that develops between Millbank and the aristocrats shows the social adjustments that must take place if England is to be united. Disraeli writes as if he had been at Eton and were a man of birth and breeding: 'political intrigue . . . [is] a dazzling practice, apt at first to fascinate youth, for it appeals at once to our invention and our courage, but one which really should only be the resource of the second-rate. Great minds must trust to great truths and great talents for their rise, and nothing else' (II, i. p. 66). That the narrator assumes the guise of a young man is important to the novel's aesthetic and argument. But it also reflects Disraeli's desperate desire to believe that his career to date was merely a prologue. Nor can we doubt the importance of this attitude as he strove for political leadership.

As a romance, as a fiction that has personal urgency to Disraeli's psyche, *Coningsby* has important continuities with the novels discussed in the first chapter. *Coningsby* is a sequel to the fantasies of youthful heroism that dominated the novels from *Vivian Grey* to *Alroy*. But the hero is no longer an outsider by temperament or nationality. In *Coningsby*, Disraeli brought the young hero to a successful climax within the political structure of England. While *The Young Duke* takes place in England, the major figure's maturation does not really lead us to believe that he will become a national leader, notwithstanding his eloquence on behalf of Catholic inclusion.

As one reads *Coningsby*, one senses Disraeli groping for the appropriate form for the political novel. He knows that he must maintain a delicate balance between public issues and historical context, on the one hand, and, on the other, the gradual development of young men who might set things right. He also understood the danger of allowing the characters through whom he expresses his ideas to become wooden. Not only Coningsby, but even Sidonia is a more complex psychological figure than has generally been realised. While at first it might seem that Disraeli has trouble focusing on his title character, the truth is otherwise. For Disraeli understood how novels unfold to readers. He realised that the process of reading about England's political turmoil would be the best way to interest his readers in the development of Coningsby from adolescent to young adult and to make them appreciate Coningsby's qualities of courage, integrity, 'high ambition', and boldness. He knew he had to establish the need for a new generation of leaders by discrediting the recent past of both Tories and Whigs and showing that idealistic younger men, untarnished by political intrigue, were emerging to govern England. Thus, he contended that since the Congress of Vienna, material advance had been accompanied by 'no proportionate advance in our moral civilisation' (II, i, p. 69). Writing of those in positions of responsibility in 1834, Disraeli remarks: 'It was this perplexed, ill-informed, jaded, shallow generation, repeating cries which they did not comprehend, and wearied with the endless ebullitions of their own barren conceit, that Sir Robert Peel was summoned to govern' (II, iv, p. 98). Perhaps Disraeli best expresses the novel's aesthetic and political creed when he says: 'Man is never so manly as when he feels deeply, acts boldly, and expresses himself with frankness and with fervour' (VII, ii, p. 350).

Coningsby remains in the background while the reader is educated in the first two Books to the need for new leadership. Disraeli's version of recent Parliamentary history and his dramatisation of the cynicism and expedience of Tadpole, Taper and Rigby refer the reader back to the promising young man introduced in the first chapter. Within the limited world of Eton, he has begun to show the qualities of courage and leadership that the nation requires. Coningsby is introduced as a magnificent figure: 'His countenance, radiant with health and the lustre of innocence, was at the same time thoughtful and resolute' (I, i, p. 2). He is contrasted with Rigby whose face 'was unhappily stamped by a sinister cast' and a demeanour which was tainted 'by an innate vulgarity' (I, i, pp. 2–3). Disraeli depicts Eton as a place where merit is recognised. When Coningsby rescues Millbank, his position as a hero is confirmed. By the end of Book Two, the question is whether Coningsby will be able to reach the status within the nation that he has achieved within the school: 'He had obtained over his intimates the ascendant power, which is the destiny of genius' (II, vii, p. 104). But to become a national leader he required wider experience and role models within the adult world.

Disraeli knew that Coningsby had to be more than a mouthpiece for his ideas. Thus, to appeal to the sympathy of his audience, he made him a 'solitary orphan'.

> The sweet sedulousness of a mother's love, a sister's mystical affection had not cultivated his early susceptibility. No soft pathos of expression had appealed to his childish ear. He was alone, among strangers, calmly and coldly kind. . . . All that he knew of the power of the softer passions might be found in the fanciful and romantic annals of schoolboy friendship. (III, i, p. 111)

Coningsby's need to be a hero at school is related to his being both an orphan from the age of nine and the neglect of his grandfather. His tearful response when he first meets his grandfather reflects his insecurity. Perhaps because he has not had intimate family relations, his quest for greatness threatens to become secondary once he falls in love: 'Ambition lost much of its splendour, even his lofty aspirations something of their hallowing impulse of paramount duty, when Coningsby felt how much ennobling delight was consistent with the seclusion of a private station' (VII, v, p. 370).

Disraeli strips Coningsby of his expectations so as to show the true quality of his character. When Coningsby accepts the loss of Edith and his grandfather's fortune, and sets himself to work hard in preparation for the bar, Disraeli renders his thoughts to demonstrate that his hero has the self-command that is the necessary prerequisite for leadership:

> Whether he inherited or forfeited fortunes, what was it to the passing throng? They would not share his splendour, or his luxury, or his comfort. But a word from his lip, a thought from his brain expressed at the right time, at the right place. . . . might change their opinions, might affect their destiny. Nothing is great but the personal. . . . Brains every day become more precious than blood. You must give men new ideas, you must teach them new words, you must modify their manners, you must change their laws, you

must root out prejudices, subvert convictions, if you wish to be great. (IX, iv, p. 455)

Disraeli was experienced enough a novelist to realise Coningsby would be far more interesting if he were not a paragon of human behaviour. Coningsby is vulnerable to jealousy; thus on slender evidence he misconstrues the friendship between Edith Millbank and Sidonia: 'He looked upon them as persons who had deeply injured him; though they really were individuals who had treated him with invariable kindness. But he felt their existence was a source of mortification and misery to him' (VI, vii, p. 334). Like Disraeli's prior heroes, Coningsby is prone to hyperbolic emotions. While sympathetic, Disraeli fully understands that his young hero is emotionally immature and must learn self-government before he can govern others. Reflecting the lessons he had learned in *Henrietta Temple* and *Venetia*, Disraeli is in full control of his aesthetic distance; for example, in one of his characteristically witty understatements, he conceals the full impact of the startling and quite temporary reversal of Coningsby's feelings towards Sidonia: 'It is quite impossible to conceal that Coningsby had imbibed for Sidonia a certain degree of aversion, which, in these days of exaggerated phrase might even be described as hatred' (VII, i, p. 344).

If Disraeli the man of action imagines himself as Coningsby, Disraeli the artist views himself as Sidonia, the Jewish polymath who sees more profoundly than his fellows. If Coningsby embodies the romance of youthful political success, Sidonia is the romance of the Jewish outsider who, despite having no position in government, is one of the most important, sophisticated, and knowledgeable figures in all Europe. His is a role that Disraeli enjoys imagining. Brilliant, worldly and influential, he becomes Coningsby's intellectual guide. Sidonia articulates Disraeli's creed; Coningsby evolves into the man who will carry it out. Often Coningsby articulates ideas that he has learned directly from Sidonia; in turn, they become the thoughts of Coningsby's friends and followers. Sidonia enables Disraeli to dramatise Coningsby's education within the novel's action; for Coningsby is profoundly affected by his conversations with a man who not only knows the history of civilisation but is familiar with the intricacies and secrets of every European government. Moreover, Sidonia enables Disraeli to make provocative statements without fully committing himself to them. Not every Tory member, including those who might be sympathetic to Young England on some issues, would have been pleased to read Sidonia's assertation that 'The tendency of advanced civilisation is in truth to pure Monarchy. . . . Your House of Commons, that has absorbed all other powers in the State, will in all probability fall more directly than it rose' (V, viii, p. 303). Through Sidonia he not only establishes the position of Jews, but acknowledges his own Jewish heritage. His readers would have recognised immediately that the first three letters of Sidonia's name reversed the author's and that Sidonia, like his creator, had a three-syllable name with the accent on the second syllable. Disraeli describes Sidonia the way he himself might have been described by one who was favourably disposed to him:

> He was . . . of a distinguished air and figure; pale, with an impressive brow, and dark eyes of great intelligence. . . . He spoke in a voice of remarkable clearness; and his manner, though easy, was touched by a degree of dignity that was engaging. (III, i, p. 114)

Sidonia instils in Coningsby the belief that a young man can be a great leader and that heroism and greatness are possibilities for him. Like Winter in *Contarini*, he delivers advice in shibboleths and abstractions; for example, 'Nurture your mind with great thoughts. To believe in the heroic makes heroes' (III, i, p. 120).

Sidonia is a more psychologically complex character than has been realised. Because he is excluded from participation in the political processes, he can only be, as he puts it, 'a dreamer of dreams' (III, i, p. 120). He regrets that he cannot be part of the life of action. Given the quality of English political institutions in the novel, the nation can certainly not afford to exclude a man of Sidonia's calibre. Disraeli illustrates the potential loss to England of excluding Jews; he knows that except for his father's having had him converted, he would not have been permitted to take his seat in Parliament.

Sidonia deserves sympathy for another reason. He cannot find love and intimacy, partly because he will not compromise his racial purity. But Disraeli gives Sidonia a more serious problem: 'He was a man without affections. It would be harsh to say he had no heart, for he was susceptible of deep emotions, but not for individuals. . . . Woman was to him a toy, man a machine' (IV, x, p. 217). In fact, his subsequent behaviour to Lucretia and his friendship to Coningsby belie this generalisation. While he does withhold himself from the rituals of courtship and avoids the kind of zealous pursuit of heterosexual love that motivates Coningsby or Egremont, his departure from Lucretia makes us realise that Disraeli's analyses do not always do justice to Sidonia's psychosexual complexity. In a melancholy scene, Sidonia asserts to Lucretia that his life is 'useless'.

If *Coningsby* were written, as Disraeli claimed, simply 'to vindicate the just claims of the Tory Party to be the popular political confederation of the country', it would be, at best, only partially successful.[18] Yet *Coningsby* is a novel that improves with each rereading, and when read in conjunction with *Sybil*, it is a splendid work. In a sense, *Sybil* 'completes' *Coningsby*; by illustrating the discontent and deprivation of the common people, the later novel implies the need for new leadership. Our minds revert to Coningsby and his friends who are gradually developing their potential for leadership during the 1837–41 period and who, we realise, represent the hope of England far more than the transitory 'three good harvests' with which *Sybil* ends. Despite its great caricatures and its incisive analyses of characters and politics, *Coningsby* is less effectual than *Sybil* because its intellectual and moral abstractions at times lack dramatic correlatives. Sidonia tells Coningsby that England's 'character as a community' has declined, and that the contemporary period is 'an age of social disorganisation' when 'the various classes of this country are arrayed against each other' (*Coningsby*, IV, xiii, pp. 237–8). But these ideas, like so many of Sidonia's oracular comments, are not *illustrated* within the narrative of *Coningsby*. It remains for *Sybil* to illustrate how men lacking adequate political and spiritual leaders may totemise their own worst instincts in the form of a savage chieftain like the Wodgate Bishop; how Chartism appeals to men who feel a void in their lives; and how the Church has become virtually a hollow anachronism. Egremont perceives rural poverty for himself in the town of Marney and sees the effect of urban industrialisation on craftsmen such as Warner. While Egremont is able to empathise with the plight of the common people as he becomes aware of their economic deprivation and while he takes a superb stand in Parliamentary debate, he lacks the magnetism and ambition to lead.

As we shall see in the next chapter, the inclusive structure of *Sybil* supplements the effects of Egremont's personal experience by presenting representative vignettes of life in England. Rapid alternation between scenes of luxury and scenes of poverty calls attention to the discrepancy between the idle, luxurious lives of the aristocracy and the struggle for economic and moral survival of the common people. The narrator of *Sybil* does not, like the narrator of *Coningsby*, restrict his interest to those possessing wealth and position or to those who serve them. His panorama includes scenes that explicitly reveal the failure of political leadership to provide for the people. For example, his voice rises in indignation and outrage as he recalls the 'penury and disease' of the 'miserable population' of Marney who are consigned to unsanitary hovels (*Sybil*, II, iii, pp. 60–2).

Tancred develops some of the social and political themes begun in *Coningsby* and *Sybil*. Tancred journeys to Jerusalem after convincing himself of the superficiality of contemporary English civilisation and the futility of its politics. The political world of the Middle East parodies the intrigues of English politics; the major difference is that weapons rather than votes are the method of settling political disagreements. Syria's 'history' parodies England's: civil war followed the deposition of a strong monarch and, when the feudal (or territorial) system was endangered, monarchist sentiments revived. In the Lebanese mountains, Tancred discovers the mirror of Young England's dreams: 'a proud, feudal aristocracy; a conventual establishment. . . . a free and armed peasantry. . . . [and] bishops worthy of the Apostles' (*Tancred*, IV, xii, p. 338). Predictably, the Young Syria Movement appeared in 1844 to 'profess nationality as their object' and to plead for 'the restoration of the house of Shehaab' (*Tancred*, V, i, p. 349). And Fakredeen epitomises the cynical aristocrats and hypocritical politicians of *Coningsby* and *Sybil* who, while espousing principles, practise self-interest. The narrator tells us that 'It was his profession and his pride to simulate and to dissemble' (III, vi, p. 214). Although he is temporarily enraptured by Tancred's plans, he lacks the moral energy to adhere to a consistent code of conduct, and once he considers the benefits of a dynasty founded on a marriage between himself and Astarte, he is not troubled by his betrayal of Tancred.

But, despite superficial resemblances to its predecessors, *Tancred* does not function as the climactic volume of the political trilogy. Originally conceived as a novel about reviving the sacred position of the Anglican Church by means of rediscovering its spiritual principles, *Tancred* becomes, whether Disraeli intended it or not, a kind of clumsy metaphor for the discovery of the divine within oneself. Anticipating a later member of a self-conceived elect, Lawrence's Rupert Birkin, Tancred discovers potential within himself but rather arbitrarily notices a dearth of both vitality and spirituality in everyone else: 'Individuality is dead; there is a want of inward and personal energy in man; and that is what people feel and mean when they go about complaining there is no faith' (*Tancred*, II, xiv, p. 147).

Tancred is a fictional version of the Victorian spiritual autobiography, epitomised by Newman's *Apologia*, Carlyle's *Sartor Resartus* and Tennyson's *In Memoriam*. Along with *Tancred*, several examples of the genre were published within a few years, including Charles Kingsley's *Yeast* (1848), James Anthony Froude's *Shadows of the Clouds* (1847), and Newman's *Loss and Gain* (1848). Mimesis in *Tancred* is based on entirely different assumptions from the rest of the trilogy. As in *Popanilla* and *Alroy*, verisimilitude of time and space is virtually absent. *Tancred* reflects Disraeli's continued admiration for romance plots. Like Byron's heroes, Childe Harold and Don Juan, or Scott's heroes in his historical romances, Tancred inhabits an imagined world where diurnal details rarely intrude into his quest.[19] An imaginary voyage, *Tancred* is loosely held together by the hero's physical journey which introduces him to incredible people and fantastic places. The novel begins in the present tense in England, but Tancred's crusade is virtually a journey backward in time; he discovers remote cultures which have religious beliefs and political customs that were in 1847 regarded condescendingly by Christian England: Judaism, pagan worship of the Greek gods, and feudalism.

Disraeli may well have believed that the art of *Tancred* demonstrated the 'imagination' that was lacking in England. As Blake notes, 'Disraeli . . . belongs to the same strand in nineteenth-century English thought as Coleridge and Carlyle, the romantic, conservative, organic thinkers who revolted against Benthamism and the legacy of eighteenth-century rationalism.'[20] As early as *Popanilla*, *Contarini Fleming* and *Alroy*, we can see his distrust of excessive logic and reason. In *Sybil*, Morley illustrates the emptiness of utilitarianism; once his own private designs are thwarted, the greatest good for the greatest number has little appeal, and repressed and unacknowledged atavistic impulses manifest themselves. The narrator in *Tancred* continually mocks scientific methodology and its inductive method, and implicitly proposes faith and intuition as superior alternatives. Lady Constance's explanation of evolution, drawn from a book she has read entitled *The Revelations of Chaos*, is a scathing indictment of the kind of scientific determinism Disraeli loathed. When Tancred dourly objects, 'I do not believe I ever was a fish', she responds: 'Everything is proved; by geology, you know' (*Tancred*, II, ix, p. 110).

Tancred is the most introspective of the trilogy's heroes, a man who confides in no one and bears the burdens of self-consciousness most acutely; neither drawing room activities nor contemporary political issues of the day interest him. As a Romantic hero, he pursues what Geoffrey H. Hartman calls 'the lure of false ultimates' in the expectation that he will find a 'final station for the mind'.[21] Tancred *never* finds the resting place he seeks. The process of searching for 'ultimates' is his consuming activity. Because he does not really find solace or direction from the angel's visitation, the novel's second half dissolves into a spiritual myth of Sisyphus where each new adventure puts him back at the start.

That the angel's revelation is not tested as a viable system is a failure of *Tancred* which severely affects the argument of the entire trilogy. The novel does not explore the meaning of the angel's message as a plausible alternative to political intrigue in Asia or to the decline of the monarchy and the church in England. Disraeli's dramatisation of Tancred's communion with the angel reflects the compelling urge to experience the presence of a higher being which permeated the Victorian period.[22] It should be noted that Tancred's quest is not as bizarre as it seems. As Halevy notes, when writing about religious questions in the 1840s, 'The belief was beginning to spread in British Protestant circles that the Second Advent of Jesus to judge the living and the dead must be preceded by a return of the Jews to Jerusalem, and the rebuilding of Solomon's Temple that on the very spot where the Saviour had been crucified they might be confuted, converted and pardoned'.[23] Disraeli's readers would have thought it was particularly appropriate that Tancred discovers the Jewish origins of Christianity in Jerusalem. But the shibboleth of theocratic equality does not justify the angel's appearance, and the angel's words are vague, if not bathetic:

> The equality of man can only be accomplished by the sovereignty of God. The longing for fraternity can never be satisfied but under the sway of a common father. The relations between Jehovah and his creatures can be neither too numerous nor too near. In the increased distance between God and man have grown up all those developments that have made life mournful. Cease, then, to seek in a vain philosophy the solution of a social problem that perplexes you. Announce the sublime and solacing doctrine of theocratic equality. (*Tancred*, IV, vii, p. 291)

Tancred becomes a ludicrous parody of, rather than – as Disraeli intended – an heir of those biblical heroes to whom God and his angels spoke.

VI

The progressive dubiety implied by each successive ending shows how Disraeli gradually abandoned the optimism with which he began the Young England novels. By the next-to-last chapter, Coningsby had discovered a political creed and demonstrated to himself that he had the capacity to represent and lead his followers. The heroic potential of Coningsby and the idealism and conduct of both Coningsby and his followers imply affirmative answers to the questions posed by the novel's closing paragraph:

> They stand now at the threshold of public life. They are in the leash, but in a moment they will be slipped. What will be their fate? Will they maintain in august assemblies and high places the great truths which, in study and in solitude, they have embraced? . . . Will they remain brave, single, and true; refuse to bow before shadows and worship phrases; sensible of the greatness of their position, recognize the greatness of their duties; denounce to a perplexed and disheartened world the frigid theories of a generalising age that have destroyed the individuality of man, and restore the happiness of their country by believing in their own energies, and daring to be great? (*Coningsby*, IX, vii, p. 477)

Despite the symbolic marriage between rich and poor, *Sybil* does not permanently resolve economic inequality or deal with the spiritual drought of the common people; nor does it show how such necessary political changes as the revival of a strong monarchy and of an independent, responsible aristocracy will take place. Neither Egremont's position as a back-bencher nor the temporary upturn in agriculture really answers *Sybil's* concluding prayer for a 'free monarchy, and a privileged and prosperous People' (*Sybil*, VI, iii, p. 489). And *Tancred*, as we have seen, ends inconclusively without establishing the dramatic correlative for its theological message.

Occasionally, the search for organic form leads critics to *impose* rigid structures and patterns where perhaps an acknowledgment of discontinuity and variety seems more apt. We should not be surprised, then, to discover Richard Levine arguing that 'the assumed later marriage of Tancred and Eva' represents 'the union between West and East'.[24] But we must recall that Eva faints and does not respond to Tancred's proposal, and Tancred has vowed never to return to England. Richard A. Levine argues that *Tancred* is the third stage of a process begun with *Coningsby* and *Sybil*. The earlier stages, according to Levine, are the realignment and solidification of the aristocracy, in which the Millbanks are depicted as equal to the Egremonts and Coningsbys, and the revival of a responsible aristocracy which recognises its duties to the people: 'This third stage in the sequence of events which will ultimately reinvigorate England must move to an area greater than politics and at the same time to one capable of giving real meaning and great principles to political parties and political action.'[25] But how will Tancred's dogma of Asian spirituality or the possible marriage to Eva *effect* change in Europe or Asia? Both Eva and her father are constantly enmeshed in intrigues and machinations. That Tancred must retreat when leading Astarte's warriors does not bode well for the project of conquering the world in the name of theocratic equality. While Egremont and Coningsby discover the values that are essential for new leadership, Tancred abandons his English values and European heritage.

Tancred, begun as an effort to reinvigorate spiritual values in England, really demonstrates Disraeli's disillusionment with Young England as a political movement. The hope voiced in *Coningsby* and *Sybil* has at best been partially fulfilled, for *Tancred* shows that so far the new generation of leaders is not yet governing. It is painfully evident that political progress has been relatively slow. When Tancred meets Coningsby, the latter seems to be engaged in the rather disappointing if not cynical activities of 'cultivating' his alliances (*Tancred*, II, viii, p. 101). When Egremont reappears in *Tancred*, he has not only chosen not to be a Cabinet member but is described as a man 'of fine mind rather than of brilliant talents' who *requires* the 'directing sympathy' of Coningsby (*Tancred*, II, xii, p. 139). It is very significant that Disraeli has Tancred renounce a parliamentary career when he meets Lord Marney (Egremont) and Coningsby, the heroes of the preceding volumes, who have predicted their hopes on rejuvenating England's political system.

That Tancred becomes a fanatic, alternating between moments of meditation and spasms of frenetic activity when he is ready to sacrifice human life for his vague dreams, reflects Disraeli's disappointment with the demise of Young England and his frustration with his failure to obtain political power. I think, too, that Disraeli must have felt that he had not dramatised the enduring spiritual principles on which a revived Church could be based and that *Tancred* did not provide an alternative to utilitarianism, rationality and objectivity. By the time he completed *Tancred*, he would have seen with regret that as the trilogy's final novel vacillates erratically from its political moorings to its concern with faith, subjectivity and imagination, it destroys the expectation raised by *Coningsby* and *Sybil* for a major political statement based on a deft analysis of the past, a sustained indictment of the present, and a prophetic vision of the future.

Tancred is as much a continuation of *Contarini Fleming*, the semi-autobiographical novel subtitled 'A Psychological Romance', as it is of the political novels of the 1840s. In *Tancred*, Disraeli transports himself as well as his title character from the demands of politics to a fantasy world populated by virtual demigods. In a 'garden' which 'seems a paradise', Tancred discovers Eva, the perfection of beauty 'as it existed in Eden' (*Tancred*, III, vii, pp. 184, 187–88). (And Sidonia describes a character called Adam Besso to Tancred as a man who 'looks as if [he] were in the garden of Eden before the fall' [*Tancred*, II, xi, p. 126].) As I argued in Chapter 1, Disraeli needs to be seen in the context of the Romantic movement. Even in the trilogy Disraeli is a Romantic, shaping politics, religion and philosophy to conform to his own private vision. Thus Tancred's search for spiritual faith may be a disguised version of Disraeli's unconscious desire to return to his racial and spiritual origins. In Hartman's words, 'Romantic art has a function analogous to that of religion. The traditional scheme of Eden, fall and redemption merges with the new triad of Nature, self-consciousness, imagination; while the last term in both involves a kind of return to the first'.[26]

4 Art and Argument in *Sybil*

I

Disraeli returned to fiction with the specific purpose of arguing the political viewpoint of Young England. He wanted the ideas of Young England, the group which recognised him as its leader after years as an outsider, to have impact upon the governing class. Disraeli wished to use *Sybil* not only to explain but to justify his political philosophy; to do this, he needed to expose the condition of England. He believed that as a potential leader he had to be identified with clearly defined theoretical positions: 'My conception of a great statesman is of one who represents a great idea – an idea which may lead him to power; an idea with which he might identify himself; an idea he may develop; an idea which he may and can impress upon the nation.'[1] In the 1849 preface to the fifth edition of *Coningsby*, he recalled his realisation that he could 'adopt the form of fiction as the instrument to scatter his suggestions . . . [and] avail himself of a method which, in the temper of the times, offered the best chance of influencing opinion'. Published in 1845, *Sybil: or the Two Nations* was one of the most inclusive novels of English life to have been written since *Tom Jones* (1749). *Sybil's* space is co-extensive with England, its time is England's history, and its subject is the political and social circumstances of English life. Although conceived as the middle volume of the Young England trilogy of which *Coningsby* (1844) and *Tancred* (1847) are the other novels, *Sybil* is the superior work of art. Avoiding the bizarre subjectivity of *Tancred* or the drawing-room claustrophobia of *Coningsby*, *Sybil* revolves around the exposure of social conditions and the indictment of a complacent aristocracy that neglects them. Once we understand the kind of novel Disraeli wrote, we shall then understand that *Sybil* deserves to stand among the major novels of the nineteenth century.

Steeped in the tradition of Austen and Eliot, critics of the English novel feel most comfortable discussing the novel of manners and morals, with its emphasis on linear character development, its equation of social and moral maturity, and its exploration of the psychological and moral conflicts within the minds of major characters.[2] Yet an aesthetic that stresses the novel as a prose poem and, as its ultimate standard, measures the structural relationship of every incident to the protagonist's personal history is not appropriate to a kind of fiction that presents a panorama of representative social and economic episodes as its major ingredient. The historical vision of the epic novel in English (for example, *Tom Jones*, *Vanity Fair* and *Ulysses*) is secondary to the acute observation of characters' actions and decisions in situations requiring a moral response. But in novels informed by a political and/or historical thesis, characters are rendered both as unique human beings and as representatives of social and economic circumstances that shape their destinies. Of course, Stendhal, Balzac and Tolstoy wrote such novels, but it may be that most Anglo-American criticism has tried to fit similar novels like *Sybil* (and, I would argue, *The Secret Agent*, *Nostromo* and *The Plumed Serpent*) into traditions which do not quite accommodate them. It follows that the critic of these novels should consider as *aesthetic issues* the inclusiveness of the novel's vision of the imagined *Zeitgeist* and the plausibility and complexity of the insight into political tensions and economic forces. For in polemical novels such as *Sybil* the author often seeks to convey a grammar of historical cause and effect rather than a grammar of motive, and how well he does it is one valid criterion by which to judge the novel. Historical verisimilitude depends upon the author's understanding of the social and economic circumstances in which events might hypothetically take place.

In such novels, the author seeks plausibility in terms not only of character psychology, but in terms of historical explanation. Since the imagined world is a detailed, if partial, factual model, an informed reader will require a knowledge of the original historical world both to understand how the writer is transmuting fact into fiction and to see what kind of order the novelist is imposing on reality. The novelist becomes historian and the historian becomes novelist, and the two roles are inseparable. *Sybil's* status as a neglected masterpiece depends in part on its insight into the causes of Chartism and its analysis of its shortcomings, on its dissection of party politics in the 1832–44 period, and on its compelling presentation of the life of the common people.

In no other Disraeli novel are character and event so subordinated to theme. The plot of *Sybil* is organised around Charles Egremont's gradual development, but no recapitulation of the plot can do justice to the novel's cross-section of English life from 1832 through 1844. The novel opens with chapters that show bored aristocrats living a dissipated idle life. The major figure, Charles Egremont, a younger son of a family that had gradually risen in prominence subsequent to Henry VIII's seizure of the monasteries, is among the bored aristocrats. Although he is a warm, generous and impulsive character, 'Enjoyment, not ambition seemed the principle of his existence' (I, v, p. 34). Yet he is a man of enormous potential, highly intelligent and observant. His widowed mother persuades him to run for Parliament. On the understanding that he has the financial support of his brother, Lord Marney, he makes the race and wins. But Marney, an example of the benighted, selfish aristocracy which is oblivious to the needs of the common people and which has no sense of an organic community, refuses to help Egremont pay his election debts. After courting the woman who ultimately marries his brother rather than himself, because he lacks an appropriate fortune, Egremont is disgusted with the 'arrogant and frigid' aristocratic life which his brother exemplifies. To solve his financial plight Lord Marney wants his brother to marry into the Mowbray family, but Egremont is not interested.

Walking near the ruins of Marney Abbey, Egremont discovers Morley, Walter Gerard and Gerard's daughter Sybil who is planning to become a nun. The Gerards, an old Catholic family, have a legitimate claim to the Mowbray estate. But Gerard is also a worker who identifies with the people and becomes one of the leaders of the Chartist movement until he is arrested. Morley is a journalist and later a theoretician of the Chartist movement; he is attracted to Sybil and thinks of Egremont as a rival for her. He helps Gerard recover his estates by discovering a man named Hatton who is expert in such affairs. Under the identity of Franklin, Egremont goes to live near the Gerards and becomes close friends with them. After Sybil and her father go to London and lobby on behalf of the Chartist petition, she learns that Egremont is an aristocrat and becomes temporarily disaffected until he arranges for her release after she and her father are seized. Gradually Egremont learns that the people of England are divided into those that are materially comfortable and those that are not. As Egremont is educated about the real condition of England, he learns about the rural poor on his brother's estates and the urban poor created by the industrial revolution. He comes to understand that aristocratic and political life ignores the needs of a discontented and miserable population. He upholds the rights of labour in Parliament. Gerard intervenes during the riotous national strike to save the Trafford factory, which has been presented as a model of the benevolent community that industry can create; this represents to Disraeli the possibility of a union between people and property. With Hatton's help, Morley uses these riots as an occasion to locate the document sustaining Gerard's claim. Marney and Morley conveniently die in these riots, and Egremont becomes heir to Marney's estate and marries Sybil.

At the outset we should review the crucial premises that inform *Sybil*. Disraeli believed that the so-called Glorious Revolution had been the occasion for the Whigs' installing an oligarchical political system which he called the Venetian Constitution. By this he meant consultation among a group of self-interested aristocrats had replaced the monarchy in substance if not form. Disraeli believed in the possibility of great men transfiguring the imagination of the people. The myth of the political messiah recurs in each of the Young England novels. In *The Political Novel* Morris Speare notes the parallel between Disraeli and Carlyle:

> [Disraeli], like Carlyle, castigated the Nobility for their weaknesses, their dilettantism, their grotesque and time-consuming habits, the effeminacies of their 'dandies,' and the hollow and superficial knowledge of their great landowners and their womenfolk about public affairs, and the phantom and mockery of their sense of responsibility to the body politic. He went farther even than Carlyle in satirizing these foibles. With Carlyle, whose *Chartism* shows a direct influence upon *Sybil*, he saw the danger in the rise of the Chartists, and preached with him the doctrine that to the landed proprietors of his day there must return that grave sense of paternal duty, that profound authority based upon personal excellence, that willingness to undertake the leadership in the solution of grave public problems, which characterized the chiefs of the great estates, and the abbots over their country-sides in the days of the Past, when men lived under a purely paternal government.[3]

Disraeli's belief that a man could not fulfil himself in private life, but rather required a position with defined responsibilities to give life meaning, is contrary to the emphasis on private fulfilment through love or communion with nature that pervades nineteenth-century literature. As Robert Langbaum has written, 'The real man, the romanticist felt, was not to be got at through his social relations – his actions, his manners – there he was superficial, he was playing a role. The real man was to be got at when he was alone, in nature, when he was "musing" – thinking, that is, by free association – or when he was having visions or dreams'.[4] Egremont fulfils himself as a public man. Although not possessing the heroic potential or personal magnetism of Coningsby or Tancred, he is a more successful representative of the aristocratic resurgence for which Disraeli hoped, because he continually demonstrates his integrity, sympathy and judgment.

Within *Sybil*, we feel a narrowing of the distance between Egremont and the narrator, as Egremont develops into the kind of man the narrator admires. Egremont is at first an aristocratic spectator observing Sybil's world, a world from which he is excluded by virtue of class and sympathy. In the first stage of Egremont's metamorphosis after he assumes the identity of Franklin, he is rather like a Wordsworthian stereotype when he responds to the sublimity of rural life. But after his self-enforced rustication, he sympathises with the physical conditions and psychological lives of others and does not, like Coningsby at times and Tancred always, seek refuge in vague abstractions. He develops a concept of self-responsibility that places service to the people before gratification of personal desires.

After he has earned the stature of a responsible leader, Egremont's own words carry substantial weight:

> The People are not strong; the People can never be strong. Their attempts at self-vindication will end only in their suffering and confusion. It is civilization that has effected, that is effecting, this change. It is that increased knowledge of themselves that teaches the educated their social duties. There is a dayspring in the history of this nation, which perhaps those only who are on the mountain tops can as yet recognise. . . . The new generation of the aristocracy of England are not tyrants, not oppressors. . . . Their intelligence, better than that, their hearts, are open to the responsibility of their position. . . . They are the natural leaders of the People. (IV, xv, pp. 319–20)

Later, he explains that the present problem is the balance of political parties; but when that ceases, 'You will witness a development of the new mind of England which will make up by its rapid progress for its retarded action. . . . The future principle of English politics will not be a levelling principle: not a principle adverse to privileges, but favourable to their extension. It will seek to ensure equality, not by levelling the Few, but, by elevating the Many' (V, ii, p. 340). Egremont becomes a spokesman for what Marx and Engels, speaking of Young England, dismissed as the 'spectacle' of 'feudal Socialism': 'half lamentation, half lampoon; half echo of the past, half menace of the future; at times, by its bitter, witty and incisive criticism, striking the bourgeoisie to the very heart's core, but always ludicrous in its effect, through total incapacity to comprehend the march of modern history'.[5]

In *Sybil*, the novel's narrator is continually present, arguing for the possibility of the heroic mind, demonstrating the effects such minds can have on their followers, and indicating the preferability of leadership by extraordinary men to more representative forms of government. The persona is something of a vatic figure, the visionary artist whose concern is *res publica*. The narrator speaks as if his consciousness is identical with the nation's collective conscience. In the historical chapters, we feel the personal urgency of a man who identifies his own well-being with the health of his nation, which is presently undermined by 'a mortgaged aristocracy, a gambling foreign commerce, a home trade founded on a morbid competition' (I, iii, p. 24). The speaker presents himself as one motivated by the desire that he should ultimately contribute to the welfare of the British people by means of showing them that their true interest does not lie either with the Whigs or the present Tories, who under the leadership of Peel have departed from the great Tory principles and tradition. Within his consciousness is a historical perspective stretching back beyond Henry VIII to the Norman invasion. On the last pages, the narrator emphasises that while narrating the plot of *Sybil*, he has corrected and re-interpreted Whig historiography:

> In an age of political infidelity, of mean passions, and petty thoughts, I would have impressed upon the rising race not to despair, but to seek in a right understanding of the history of their country and in the energies of heroic youth, the elements of national welfare. . . . The written history of our country for the last ten reigns has been a mere phantasma; giving to the origin and consequence of public transactions a character and colour in every respect dissimilar to their natural form and hue. In this mighty

mystery all thoughts and things have assumed an aspect and title contrary to their real quality and style: Oligarchy has been called Liberty; an exclusive Priesthood has been christened a National Church; Sovereignty has been the title of something that has had no dominion, while absolute power has been wielded by those who profess themselves the servants of the People. (VI, xii, pp. 488–9)

II

Sybil represents a substantial development in Disraeli's artistry. In it, Disraeli uses the novel form to discover the potential within extant institutions and to posit their revival as a conservative alternative not only to the present condition of the Church, the monarchy and the political parties but also to the anarchy and disruption of Chartism. The Chartists wished to extend the vote to the working class (but not women). They sought to elect their own representatives to a convention in London which, as Halevy writes, 'in contrast to the members of Parliament returned by a restricted franchise, would be the genuine representatives of the people'.[6] But the Chartists also flirted with armed rebellion and roused fears of an English version of the French Revolution. From Disraeli's perspective the Chartists were the inevitable result of the failure of the Whigs' middle-class government and utilitarian philosophy to serve the common people.

The relationship between Egremont and Sybil is explored for its historical implications. For example in one crucial scene, Egremont visits Westminster Abbey and discovers Sybil there. Sybil's presence gives meaning and vitality to the church, as she had done before at Marney Abbey, and implies to Egremont that the present degradation of the Anglo-Catholic Church need only be temporary. She replaces within the Abbey the 'noisy vergers [who] sat like ticket-porters' and 'the boards and the spikes' which made the Abbey seem 'as if [it] were in a state of seige' (IV, vi, pp. 266–7). Because Charles's consciousness is synonymous with the narrator's retrospective understanding, Sybil becomes an *emblem*, within the novel's dialectic, for the potential of the Church:

The sounds, those mystical and thrilling sounds that at once exalt the soul and touch the heart, ceased; the chanting of the service recommenced; the motionless form moved; and as she moved

> Egremont came forth from the choir, and his eye was at once caught by the symmetry of her shape and the picturesque position which she gracefully occupied; still gazing through that grate, while the light, pouring through the western window, suffused the body of the church with a soft radiance, just touching the head of the unknown with a kind of halo. (IV, vi, pp. 267–8)

Ministering charity and providing spiritual encouragement, the Catholic Sybil and the Anglican vicar of Mowbray, St. Lys, demonstrate the potential of England's true religious traditions working in unison. The convent and the Mowbray Cathedral are remnants of the tradition of mercy and charity represented by Marney Abbey before the monasteries were seized by Henry VIII. (As we have seen, until the 1850s, Disraeli was sympathetic to Catholics because they too had been an ostracised minority until 1828.) By implying that the Anglican Church is not fundamentally different from the Catholic Church particularly at a time when several members of the Oxford Movement had made the journey to Rome, Disraeli was taking a controversial position. One reviewer of *Sybil* chidingly commented, the 'extinct worship of the Catholic saints is regretted'.[7] Perhaps because Disraeli in *Sybil* seemed to endorse the Tractarians, he went out of his way to dramatise Tancred's religious epiphany as a private Protestant experience. In *Tancred*, moreover, he attempted to move beyond contemporary religious politics by broadening his ecumenical spirit to include Judaism.

The Oxford Movement stood for tradition and wished to introduce rituals into the Anglican Church which were part of the Catholic service prior to the Reformation. In 1841, the members of the Movement had published the ninetieth of *Tracts for the Times*. Newman tried to show how an Anglican Protestant could subscribe to the Thirty-nine Articles of the Book of Common Prayer, but did so in terms that made clear that the rubric of that Book was not being observed by non-Tractarians as scrupulously as it should be. In writing to strengthen the waverers among the Tractarians, Newman seemed to be arguing that the Prayer Book was essentially Catholic. The result was a ferocious attack on Newman. The subsequent decline of the Oxford Movement's influence was accelerated when W. G. Ward published *The Ideal of a Christian Church* in 1844. In his *The Oxford Movement*, R. W. Church summarises Ward's arguments: 'only the Roman Church satisfies the conditions of what a

Church ought to be, and [he argued] in detail that the English Church, in spite of its professions, utterly and absolutely fails to fulfil them'.[8] Edward Pusey, Regius Professor of Hebrew, had been suspended from preaching for two years in 1843, and Newman's long rumoured conversion was soon to take place on 9 October 1845.

The Oxford Movement had parallels to Young England not only in its desire to revive the medieval church but in its nostalgia for the medieval world and its love of ceremony. As Blake has noted, 'Young England was the Oxford movement translated by Cambridge from religion into politics. Both stemmed from the same origin – an emotional revulsion against the liberal utilitarian spirit of the time'.[9] Disraeli's conception of the proper role of the Anglican Church was influenced by the Oxford Movement which like Young England was a revolt against rationalism and the Enlightenment. What A. C. Chadwick has written of the Oxford Movement is equally true of Young England: both wanted 'to find a place and value for historical tradition, against the irrelevant or sacriligious hands of critical revolutionaries for whom no antiquity was sacred. They suspected the reason of common sense as shallow. They wanted to justify order and authority in Church as well as State'.[10] Moreover, both movements thought of Charles I as a martyr and discarded the epithet 'Glorious' to describe the revolution of 1688.

At the beginning of Book V, Sybil apprehends Egremont's value when she reads his speech expressing 'immortal truths' and upholding 'the popular cause': '[He] had pronounced his conviction that the rights of labour were as sacred as those of property; that if a difference were to be established, the interests of the living wealth ought to be preferred; [he] had declared that the social happiness of the millions should be the first object of a statesman, and that, if this were not achieved, thrones and dominions, the pomp and power of the courts and empires, were alike worthless' (V, i, p. 337). While it is easy to smile at the unintended bathos when she looks up from the journal she is reading in St. James Park and finds Egremont standing before her, this is to ignore the novel's polemic aesthetic. Disraeli does show how Egremont's response to Sybil combines sexual attraction and religious adoration. The 'portrait of a saint' that he selects from his mother's collection because it suggests Sybil seems more sexual than iconographic: 'The face of a beautiful young girl, radiant and yet solemn, with rich tresses of golden brown hair, and large eyes dark as night, fringed with ebony lashes that hung upon the glowing cheek' (IV, ii, p. 242).

By dramatising how Egremont discovers Sybil's spiritual potential and how she discovers his political insight, Disraeli suggests that their possible union is significant and desirable in far more than personal terms. Because he wishes Sybil to represent the spiritual values that England requires, it is not surprising that she does not emerge as a distinct personality. It might be objected that Sybil's soul-searching about whether she should take the veil never becomes vivid, but Sybil's conflict is peripheral to Disraeli's concerns.

At times a major flaw in Disraeli's prior fiction is his unintentionally bathetic change in voice which has the effect of trivialising both the thrust of his satire and the reader's engagement with the intellectual and emotional lives of his characters.[11] But in *Sybil* rapid changes in tone are often rhetorically effective; they accompany shifts in place and do contribute to the contrast between the neglected and the over-indulged – and within the latter group, between those like Egremont who recognise their responsibility to the deprived and those like his brother and the residents of Mowbray castle who do not. By presenting a panorama of people from every class and rapidly sweeping across the geography of England, Disraeli creates an elaborate canvas where the meaning of each episode depends upon its relation to the whole. Disraeli's principal mode of rhetorical argument is the rapid juxtaposition of contrasting scenes not only from chapter to chapter, but even from paragraph to paragraph within a chapter. An example of the latter takes place in the second chapter of Book II. After establishing the beautiful landscape that might be seen approaching the rural town of Marney, the narrator readjusts the perspective of the potential visitors (and the readers) and discovers a scene of deprivation and filth. In the very next paragraph he further arouses the reader's sense of outrage by suddenly revealing that within one of these 'wretched tenements' of two rooms live three generations of a family, including a pregnant woman and a father stricken by typhoid. Later, Gerard explains to Egremont why these 'wretched tenements' exist: how Henry VIII's seizure of the monasteries permanently affected the quality of rural life; how those owning estates had destroyed rural cottages; and how absentee landlords had exploited the land for revenue.

The aristocracy's stupidity, boredom and enervation contrast both with the vitality and energy of the common people and with Egremont's developing self-awareness and understanding about his country. Egremont's opposite, his brother Lord Marney, disdains the needs of the people and represents the model that Egremont must renounce. He places self before family, family before party, and party before class. Until the last chapter's *deus ex machina* when the poor are either miraculously restored to their former position or elevated to a higher economic situation, the gradual decline of the Mowbray poor is contrasted with the stasis and ennui of aristocrats. Disraeli exposes the aristocrats' abdication of responsibility by juxtaposing the conversation of the downtrodden Londoners who congregate outside Deloraine House with that of the people attending the party inside. How can the Chartist frustration be condemned when the Members of Parliament to whom Gerard and Morley take their petition are not only uninformed but arrogant and disdainful? The names of such MPs as Wriggle and Thorough Base are self-indicting, and their conduct verifies their names. Kremlin, another MP, informs Gerard and Morley that he is uninterested in 'domestic policy' and that 'forms of government were of no consequence' (IV, v, p. 256). Only Lord Valentine receives them intelligently and courteously, even if with condescension. But unlike Egremont, Valentine has not experienced the condition of the common people firsthand and cannot comprehend the depth of their feeling.

A brief look at the first eight chapters of Book III shows Disraeli's artistry. He deftly organised his chapters so that we necessarily perceive Egremont's personal life not simply in its private moments, but also in the context of the moral and economic conditions to which it is his duty to respond. Book III oscillates rapidly from poverty to wealth, beginning with the juxtaposition of life in the mines (ch. i) to the aristocratic pretence of the Marneys (ch. ii). Both Digg's Tommy Shop (ch. iii) and Wodgate (chs. iv and vii) parody the heartless tyranny of Lord Marney as if to imply that a cynical and indifferent aristocracy inevitably affects the quality of civilisation for the entire population. While misery and degradation swirl around him, Egremont seems to have neither the means nor the desire to redress social and economic blight. For, as we have seen, he has temporarily withdrawn to an idyllic life where, under the pseudonym of Franklin, he has developed his friendship with Gerard and Sybil (chs. v and vi). Chapter vii switches back to the Bishop of Wodgate as if to emphasise the alternative leadership that is developing while Egremont eschews his responsibility. Trafford's factory (ch. viii), an example of enlightened aristocratic behaviour, explicitly suggests the need for Egremont, who has been elected a Member of Parliament, to assume his public responsibilities.

In the opening chapter of Book III, the narrator conveys his outrage and indignation as he recalls the degradation of children working in the mines:

> . . . troops of youth, alas! of both sexes, though neither their raiment nor their language indicates the difference; all are clad in male attire; and oaths that men might shudder at, issue from lips born to breathe words of sweetness. Yet these are to be, some are, the mothers of England! But can we wonder at the hideous coarseness of their language, when we remember the savage rudeness of their lives? Naked to the waist, an iron chain fastened to a belt of leather runs between their legs clad in canvas trousers, while on hands and feet an English girl, for twelve, sometimes for sixteen hours a day, hauls and hurries tubs of coals up subterranean roads, dark precipitous, and plashy; circumstances that seem to have escaped the notice of the Society for the Abolition of Negro Slavery. Those worthy gentlemen too appear to have been singularly unconscious of the sufferings of the little trappers, which was remarkable, as many of them were in their own employ. (III, i, p. 161)

Disraeli has turned his talents for elaborate description and ironic observation to graphic rendering of social evil. He has learned to use a single sentence, such as the last one in the prior passage, to point out swiftly and surely a grim social incongruity – in this case, the neglect of their own employees by those professing worthy motives and subscribing to noble causes. When the narrator in the next chapter elegises the close of an 'agreeable party' at Mowbray castle, conditions such as those depicted in the above quotation ironically undercut his prior narcissistic pose:

> The sudden cessation of all those sources of excitement which pervade a gay and well-arranged mansion in the country unstrings the nervous system. For a week or so, we have done nothing which was not agreeable, and heard nothing which was not pleasant. Our self-love has been respected; there has been a total cessation of petty cares; all the enjoyment of an establishment without any of its solicitude. We have beheld civilisation only in its favoured aspect, and tasted only the sunny side of the fruit. (III, ii, p. 168)

Disraeli's ventriloquism here has intentionally made the reader momentarily complicit in Lord Marney's selfish and infantile self-absorption. But Disraeli wants us to realise that any attempt to lyricise Marney's sense of loss becomes reductive and trivial:

> But sometimes it is not in our power; sometimes, for instance, we must return to our household gods in the shape of a nursery; and though this was not the form assumed by the penates of Lord Marney, his presence, the presence of an individual so important and so indefatigable, was still required. His lordship has passed his time at Mowbray to his satisfaction. He had had his own way in everything. His selfishness had not received a single shock. He had laid down the law and it had not been questioned. He had dogmatised and impugned, and his assertions had passed current, and his doctrines had been accepted as orthodox. (III, ii, pp. 168–9)

The entire social and political system at Wodgate – from its mock theocracy to the high-handed ruthlessness with which the 'aristocrats' treat their subjects – is an indictment of the English Church and Government which should provide moral, political and religious leadership. The savage master of the lock manufacturing enterprise is called the Bishop, and he rules not only his shop but Wodgate himself. As the brutalised youth explains to Morley, 'That's his name and authority; for he's the governor here over all of us. And it has always been so that Wodgate has been governed by a bishop; because, as we have no church, we will have as good. And by this token that his day se'nnight, the day my time was up, he married me to this here young lady' (III, iv, p. 192). If Disraeli seemed to be calling for a new feudal relationship between man and master, between worker and factory owner, between tenant and landowner, between common man and aristocrat, he felt no reason to be apologetic. He once said, 'The principle of the feudal system . . . was the noblest principle, the grandest, the most magnificent that was ever conceived by patriot'.[12] His basic premise was that the ownership of property conferred moral and economic responsibilities in regard to the poor and unfortunate.

Because even uneducated barbarians have a natural need to 'adore and obey', the Bishop and his fellow master workmen fill a vacuum in the lives of their followers which is created by the abnegation of responsibility by the aristocracy, government, and clergy: '[The Wodgate aristocracy] is distinguished from the main body not merely by name. It is the most knowing class at Wodgate; it possesses indeed in its way complete knowledge; and it imparts in its manner a certain quantity of it to those whom it guides. Thus it is an aristocracy that leads, and therefore a fact' (III, iv, p. 188). As Bishop Hatton marches at the head of the Hell-cats during the Chartist uprising, the procession is bathetically compared with 'the Pilgrimage of Grace' (VI, vi, p. 434). By viewing his procession in terms of such a historically significant religious event as the 'conversion of Constantine' (VI, vi, p. 433), Disraeli stresses the ironic disjunction between past and present – in this case, between the former dignity of the monarchy and the church and those who now 'preach' and 'control' (III, iv, p. 189).

Arthur Frietzsche has commented that Disraeli's compassion for the working class 'was never lifted above aristocratic paternalism'.[13] (At times Disraeli does tend to associate complacent vulgarity and insolence with the quality of life led by the working class, as if this were prima-facie evidence for placing faith in the leadership of a revived aristocracy.)[14] But in *Sybil*, vitality, intelligence and resourcefulness give the working class characters such as Bishop Hatton, Dandy Mick and Devilsdust the kind of energy and substance that we associate with the minor personae of Shakespeare and Dickens. Disraeli's challenge as an artist was to render the minor characters as the inevitable results of social and economic conditions that had to be changed, while simultaneously dramatising the vitality, the individuality and the essential humanity of what he regarded as England's neglected resource – the downtrodden common people. Describing the unique manners and personality of the minor characters proves less difficult for Disraeli's artistry than presenting a character as representative of a crystallising social situation. Yet he can be extremely effective in the latter, as in the case of the poor weaver, Warner, whose bewilderment and estrangement are the result of his being rendered obsolete by machinery:

> It is not vice that has brought me to this, nor indolence, nor imprudence. I was born to labour, and I was ready to labour. I loved my loom, and my loom loved me. It gave me a cottage in my native village, surrounded by a garden, of whose claims on my solicitude it was not jealous. There was time for both. It gave me for a wife the maiden that I had ever loved; and it gathered my children round my hearth with plenteousness and peace. I was content: I sought no other lot. It is not adversity that makes me look back upon the past with tenderness.
>
> Then why am I here? Why am I, and six hundred thousand

subjects of the Queen, honest, loyal, and industrious, why are we, after manfully struggling for years, and each year sinking lower in the scale, why are we driven from our innocent and happy homes, our country cottages that we loved, first to bide in close towns without comforts, and gradually to crouch into cellars, or find a squalid lair like this, without even the common necessaries of existence; first the ordinary conveniences of life, then raiment, and at length food, vanishing from us. (II, xiii, p. 133)

If we were to read the above remarks as a psychic gesture of Warner's inner life they would seem artificial and stylised. The movement from 'I' to 'we' obviously stresses that Warner typifies an economic situation for which he is the novel's spokesman. But Warner's set speech is part of the evolving indictment of a society which neglects its working poor. Within the novel's polemic, the speech is an implicit comment on a conversation in the previous chapter between Lord Marney and St. Lys. As is his custom, Marney takes refuge in theories and abstractions that confirm his prejudices and justify his stinginess: 'I have generally found the higher the wages the worse the workman. They only spend their money in the beer-shops. *They* are the curse of this country' (III, xii, p. 127; emphasis Disraeli's).

More consistently than in his prior novels, wit and paradox are an intrinsic part of the novel's themes. For example, speaking of two aristocratic brothers, Disraeli has his narrator remark: 'Both had exhausted life in their teens, and all that remained for them was to mourn, amid the ruins of their reminiscences, over the extinction of excitement' (I, i, p. 3). Disraeli never wrote an opening that approached the brilliance of the opening chapters of *Sybil*. The scene in a 'golden saloon' prior to a major horse race captures the prodigality, the misplaced spasms of energy alternating with boredom, and the dissipation of lives and resources wasted in the pursuit of narcissistic pleasure that characterises aristocratic life. The participants are oblivious to the Chartist storm of dissatisfaction and protest gathering over their heads. The race becomes a metaphor for the political struggle between two parties that lack any purpose or principle other than their own survival. The horse race is depicted in language that would be more appropriate to a major historical event; the incongruity between the language and the object of description stresses how far the aristocracy has strayed from its historic heritage;

A few minutes, only a few minutes, and the event that for twelve

> months has been the pivot of so much calculation, of such subtle combinations, of such deep conspiracies, round which the thought and passion of the sporting world have hung like eagles, will be recorded in the fleeting tablets of the past. . . . Finer still, the inspired mariner who has just discovered a new world; the sage who has revealed a new planet; and yet the 'Before' and 'After' of a first-rate English race, in the degree of its excitement, and sometimes in the tragic emotions of its close, may vie even with these. (I, i, p. 9)

Like the aristocrats in Pope's *The Rape of the Lock*, these men have confused trivial with important matters.

III

It is a curiosity of *Sybil* that the basic theme, the division between the wealthy and the poor, is articulated by Morley – Egremont's amoral, agnostic and paranoid rival who foresees the decline of family: 'Two nations; between whom there is no intercourse and no sympathy; who are as ignorant of each other's habits, thoughts, and feelings, as if they were dwellers in different zones, or inhabitants of different planets; who are formed by a different breeding, are fed by a different food, are ordered by different manners, and are not governed by the same laws' (I, v, p. 76). It is part of the novel's subtlety to show that perspicacity is not the province of the well-meaning characters alone. If at first Morley seems to be Disraeli's spokesman, we should remember that (i) his rational analysis provides no solution; (ii) he lacks imagination, sympathy and manners; (iii) his abstractions are often not sustained by the action; (iv) his disregard for the past is contradictory to Disraeli's beliefs; and (v) Morley's attempt to murder his rival and implicitly to barter his father's safety for Sybil's declaration of love for him completely discredits him. Ultimately, by showing the possibilities of bridging the schism between rich and poor by the merger of Sybil and Egremont, Disraeli refutes Morley's view that the division could not be breached. (Yet how much more effective the novel's resolution would have been – and how shocking to Disraeli's Victorian audience – if Sybil did not have an aristocratic heritage!)

Disraeli gradually changes the reader's mind about Morley. While Egremont grows in knowledge, feeling and judgment, Morley contracts in stature when he is shown to be motivated by venomous class hatred. Disraeli has learned to show how a character learns from experience. While in past novels, characters have a kind of conversion experience following a major event (the Young Duke's riotous night of gambling, Vivian's killing a man in a duel, the death of Contarini's wife), in this novel an accretion of important events gradually changes Egremont. This kind of character development, used only by Austen in the English novel prior to Disraeli, is a cornerstone of the later nineteenth-century realistic novel and its successor, the twentieth-century psychological novel.

The narrator re-educates the reader to understand that Morley's reductive view of the irrevocable division between the privileged and the people derives from paranoid class hatred. Even if no permanent solution to economic disparity is dramatised within the novel, Trafford's benevolent capitalism, as well as Egremont's ever-expanding perspicacity and willingness to speak in Parliament for the poor, is meant to refute Morley's view that the schism between rich and poor is inevitable. Morley's faith in progress is a parody of the material determinism of Robert Owens and of the Victorian cliché (which Disraeli rejected) that new and better institutions will continue to evolve:

> The domestic principle has fulfilled its purpose. The irresistible law of progress demands that another should be developed. It will come; you may advance or retard, you cannot prevent it. It will work out like the development of organic nature. In the present state of civilisation, and with the scientific means of happiness at our command, the notion of home should be obsolete. Home is a barbarous idea; the method of a rude age: Home is isolation; therefore anti-social. What we want is Community. (III, ix, p. 223)

Disraeli would have expected his Victorian audience to recognise that there is something fundamentally wrong with a character who questions that most sacrosanct cornerstone of Victorian life, the family. Disraeli effectively undermines Morley when he has Gerard rather touchingly respond, 'but I like stretching my feet on my own hearth' (III, ix, p. 223). In the Victorian period, the family was equated with home which was, as Houghton has written, 'both a shelter *from* the anxieties of modern life, a place of peace where the longings of the soul might be realized (if not in fact, in imagination), and a shelter *for* those moral and spiritual values which the commercial spirit and the critical spirit were threatening to destroy, therefore also a sacred place, a temple'[15] (emphases Houghton's). The agnostic Morley is revealed as a fundamentally amoral character who would aid Gerald only if *paid* with Sybil's affections. Admiringly, he tells Baptist Hatton, a man whose ruthlessness and expediency resemble his own: 'You have a clear brain and a bold spirit; you have no scruples, which indeed are generally the creatures of perplexity rather than of principle' (V, xi, p. 398). As if to emphasise the mechanistic nature of the utilitarian Morley, Disraeli has him assault Egremont with his 'iron grasp' and 'hand of steel' (III, x, p. 232). Morley's motive is sexual jealousy rather than fanatical commitment to any social values. At Morley's death, Disraeli stresses the ironic discrepancy between Morley's apparent idealism and actual behaviour; his narrator relates how, with the name of Sybil on his lips, 'the votary of Moral Power and the Apostle of Community ceased to exist' (VI, xii, p. 482).

Yet *Sybil* ends not with a prediction but with a prayer:

> That we may live to see England once more possess a free Monarchy, and a privileged and prosperous People is my prayer; and that these great consequences can only be brought about by the energy and devotion of our Youth is my persuasion. We live in an age when to be young and to be indifferent can no longer be synonymous. We must prepare for the coming hour. The claims of the Future are represented by suffering millions: and the Youth of a Nation are the trustees of Posterity. (V, xiii, p. 489)

The narrator has the perspicacity to analyse England's problems. But he suggests no programme for ameliorating the spiritual and moral condition of England, because neither Disraeli nor Young England had a coherent political programme. The novel's conclusion does not eradicate the intense analysis of the effects of industrialisation, mediocre government or irresponsible landlords. The deaths of Morley and Bishop Hatton do not solve England's underlying problems. Yet, if the novel does not dramatise a revival of ceremony and form, a restoration of the position of the Church, or the ascent to power of an enlightened aristocracy, it does show the potential within England of creative sympathy among the classes, the desire of the people for strong charismatic leadership, and a feudal alternative to a centralised government that imposes its laws from London. Because the conclusion lacks the intensity of the chapters at Wodgate and at the mines, one suspects that the 'three good harvests' that follow the resolution of the plot are nothing more than a temporary cycle in the *economic* plight of the miners and the agrarian poor not so fortunate to have Egremont as their landlord. (Earlier, the narrator obliquely had expressed Disraeli's continuing concern that economic prosperity might damage the moral and spiritual condition of the people: '[The system of Dutch Finance] has so overstimulated the energies of the population to maintain the material engagements of the state, and of society at large, that the moral condition of the people has been entirely lost sight of' [I, iii, p. 24].)

Certainly too much has been made of Disraeli's optimism. For example, in *The Victorian Sage*, John Holloway writes:

> [Disraeli] was an optimist about both the quality of life, and its ultimate results: he saw the world as an exciting, exhilarating place, and a place that characteristically supplied happy endings. . . . There is no inescapable contrast between what is and what should be. . . . Disraeli does not explore that part of human experience which comprises sin, guilt, depravity, or misfortune; they are not primary data in the view of life which his work conveys.[16]

This view does not do justice to the implications of Disraeli's art in *Sybil*. Like *Bleak House, Sybil* does not constrain or ameliorate the malevolent social forces that blight the quality of English life. Even more than *Bleak House, Sybil* opens up the dark side of Victorian England, the side revealed in the Blue Books.[17] Whereas in *Bleak House* the omniscient narrator's panorama of disease, injustice and grinding poverty alternates with Esther's private journal of personal development and fulfilment, in *Sybil* the historical and sociological perspective pushes relentlessly forward as it satirises aristocratic pretensions and exposes the discrepancy between those who labour to survive and those who live an idle, luxurious life. Disraeli the novelist is more honest than Disraeli the theoretician of Young England. Hence the novel ends with a tentative conclusion rather than rhetorical optimism. Disturbing facts of economic life and troubling aspects of aristocratic life are not resolved by Egremont's marriage to Sybil. The novel leaves the polemic of the early chapters behind. The power and specificity of the women and children working in the mine; of the gradual decline in working class prosperity in Mowbray, as evidenced by 'The Temple of the Muses' and Mrs Carey; of the misery in the Warner household; of the turbulence created by rural and urban poverty; and of the desperation of the Chartist petition – all these undermine Disraeli's more parochial political diatribes, particularly such partisan oversimplifications as 'Whiggism was putrescent in the nostrils of the nation' (I, iii, p. 22).

Georg Lukaçs' praise of the great nineteenth-century realists, Balzac and Tolstoy, is appropriate to Disraeli's artistry in *Sybil*:

> If, therefore, in the process of creation their conscious world-view comes into conflict with the world seen in their vision, what really emerges is that their true conception of the world is only superficially formulated in the consciously held world-view and the real depth of their *Weltanschauung*, their deep ties with the great issues of their time, their sympathy with the sufferings of the people can find adequate expression only in the being and fate of their characters.[18]

The marriage between Egremont and Sybil – after seemingly impossible obstacles are overcome by an unlikely plot – is not the apocalypse that Disraeli seems to have intended, because the lives of Egremont and Sybil remain peripheral to and are transcended by Disraeli's moving presentation of the exploitation in the mines, the degradation of Wodgate, and the recurring threat of rural and urban deprivation.

5 The Argument and Significance of Disraeli's Last Novels

I

Disraeli's final novels, *Lothair* (1870) and *Endymion* (1880), are generally consigned to oblivion or treated as footnotes to his later years as a political figure. Not only has their merit been ignored, but their importance to students of Disraeli and the Victorian era has been underestimated.[1] *Lothair* is Disraeli's last effort to cope with the pluralism and dubiety which was becoming so much a part of Victorian life in the late 1860s, while his final novel *Endymion* is an elder statesman's nostalgic reminiscence of what seemed the less complex period of his youth. The Reform Bill of 1867 with its extension of the franchise, the Hyde Park demonstrations in favour of extending the franchise, the insurrection and brutal suppression in Jamaica in 1865, and the subsequent trial of the British Governor of that colony, the financial crisis of 1866, the controversy over Irish Disestablishment, and the concomitant disturbances about Irish matters, all made the 1860s a particularly turbulent period. As Ian Gregor has noted, the 'uneasiness, so general a characteristic of these years', found expression not only in Arnold's *Culture and Anarchy*, but in Bagehot's *The English Constitution*, Marx's *Das Kapital* and Carlyle's *Shooting Niagara: And After?*.[2]

Disraeli addresses many of the same contemporary intellectual issues raised by Newman's *Apologia* (1864) and Arnold's *Culture and Anarchy* (1869): the position of the Anglican Church in England; the respective roles of individual conscience, authority and faith in determining one's religious views; and the moral and spiritual responsibilities of the English aristocracy. Yet in these novels he is less interested in polemics and more interested in mankind's infinite variety.

Disraeli had ceased writing novels when his imagination found an outlet in directing and organising his own career, his political party, and the legislative issues before the House of Commons. When we learn of Disraeli's involvement in the political manipulations that preceded the Second Reform Bill (1867), and see him savouring his role as an historic figure, another side of his creativity emerges.[3] If ever a man created an identity it was Disraeli. As Walter Bagehot remarked, 'Mr. Disraeli owes his great success to his very unusual capacity for *applying* a literary genius in itself quite limited to the practical purposes of public life' (emphasis Bagehot's).[4] Bagehot helps us to understand how and why Benjamin Disraeli's literary and political careers often prospered alternately. He returned to novel writing during the six year period (1868–74) between his two terms as Prime Minister and again after he had left office in 1880. Probably he resumed novel writing when he was out of office because his creative energies required an outlet. Disraeli's last novels rediscover the imagination, playfulness and fantasy that had become increasingly submerged during his political odyssey. In these novels, it may be that the creative process – the activity of making fiction – became as important to him as the subject of his fiction, just as the processes of governing and the art of gaining and holding power intrigued him as much as his political goals.

Disraeli's later novels are radical departures from the Young England trilogy of the 1840s that sought to urge a moral and political reformation, while articulating the political and spiritual values on which he wished to predicate his career. In contrast to the trilogy of the 1840s, these novels do not try to propose a coherent political programme or religious philosophy.[5] Unlike the dramatisation of political and social views in *Coningsby* and *Sybil*, where the correctness or errors of the political views that a character holds are often (but not always, as *Sybil*'s Morley illustrates) an index of the character of the man who holds them, in *Lothair*, Disraeli tentatively and dispassionately explores major nineteenth-century epistemological positions. He also resumes his interest in character psychology that we saw in the novels of the 1820s and 1830s, but he does so from the perspective of an objective mature observer of the quirks and idiosyncrasies of human behaviour.

In Disraeli's novels prior to the 1840s trilogy, his interest in character psychology was most prominent when he wrote of Romantic protagonists whom he imagined as surrogates for himself, as he did in *Vivian Grey*, *Contarini Fleming* and *Alroy*. In his early novels, Disraeli had difficulty in detaching himself sufficiently from his protagonists to examine them as fully developed human beings. Because he could not move from immersion to reflection, they turned out to be thinly veiled versions of himself. The trilogy of the 1840s became a means for Disraeli to articulate the political and spiritual values on which he wished to predicate his public career. Not only did age and experience mellow his Byronic impulses, but the Victorian novel's masterful use of the omniscient narrator to probe characters' psyches and its focus on the darker recesses of the mind undoubtedly affected his art in his last two novels. The increased subtlety of Disraeli's character psychology in these novels typifies the developing Victorian awareness – particularly in Browning, George Eliot and, later, Hardy – of the distinction between the public self that one presents to the world and the barely understood, dimly acknowledged private self. Yet since Disraeli had spent his career reconciling disparate aspects of his psyche, and knew from his own experience how the private self had demands that were incongruous with his public identity, he was a precursor of this awareness. In his last novels Disraeli objectively and detachedly examines the psyche of his characters – particularly some of the secondary characters – in terms of obsessions, fixations and compulsions that heretofore were unrecognised in his novels. Even in *Endymion*, which like the earlier works mimes aspects of his life, he is often fascinated with the human psyche for its own sake.

II

Lothair's popularity can be attributed not only to Disraeli's status as a former Prime Minister, but to its anti-Catholicism. Contemporary readers would have recognised his references to the conversion of the Marquess of Bute which intensified the pervasive anxiety that the Anglican Church would be rent by an exodus to Catholicism.[6] Disraeli is concerned that one of the pillars of the English social and political system, the Anglican Church, is variously threatened by Catholicism, popular political movements and atheism. He had convinced himself that Irish Disestablishment was a threat to the national Church in England. His own disillusionment with Roman Catholicism had been intensified in 1868 because he not only felt that he had been betrayed by Archbishop Manning (the model for Cardinal Grandison) whose support he had obtained for a Catholic

University subsidy before Gladstone won Manning's favour by sponsoring Irish Disestablishment, but he also probably resented the Roman Catholics for causing the difficulties in Ireland which led to his downfall.[7] That the England depicted by Disraeli in *Lothair* is torn by religious dissension and is lacking in political direction reflects some bitterness over his last tumultuous months as Prime Minister in 1868. After all, Disraeli had lost office in the 1868 election *because* Gladstone had come out clearly for the Disestablishment of the Anglican Church in Ireland and was supported in that position by Disraeli's ally, Manning, who abandoned Disraeli as soon as he saw that the Liberals under Gladstone would do better for the Catholics.

It is not the dogma of the Anglican Church with which he is concerned, but the substantial contribution that a national Church with allegiance only to the Crown and to the people makes to England's political health. Even prior to this, Disraeli had come to see the value of a national Church: 'Broadly and deeply planted in the land, mixed up with all our manner and customs, one of the main guarantees of our local government, and therefore of our common liberties, the Church of England is part of our history, part of our life, part of England itself'.[8] Although Disraeli owed the Church only pro forma allegiance, the possibility of England's losing part of the common social denominator that defined its political order seemed quite real. From Disraeli's point of view, the problem of religious pluralism is that it causes both conflict and doubt within the populace. When Corisande says 'I frequently feel that some great woe is hanging over our country', or when she makes the melancholy remark that 'All seems doubt and change, when it would appear that we require both faith and firmness', she represents Disraeli's feeling in 1870 that a national Church is a catalyst for political unity and for the moral health that Disraeli believed would follow from political unity (*Lothair*, ch. xii, pp. 50–1). While *Lothair* covers the period from August 1866 to August 1868, it ostentatiously omits reference to the Reform Bill and to political activity during the period when Disraeli played such a prominent role. But the title character is a kind of educated Everyman testing major nineteenth-century moral, religious and political positions. He is at the centre of a morality play and characters espousing Roman Catholicism, Anglicanism, Hellenism and Republicanism try to woo him to their position. But *Lothair* is Disraeli's ideological *Pilgrim's Progress*, even if it does not conclusively dramatise the desideratum of the title character's quest as he oscillates from position to position.

The title character of *Lothair* is an orphan who succeeds to a huge inheritance on his twenty-first birthday. His father had appointed as his guardians his Scotch Presbyterian uncle, Lord Cullodan, and Cardinal Grandison, a convert whom he had not met before but who wishes to convert Lothair to Catholicism. The book opens at Brentham where Lothair is not only captivated by the gracious, if somewhat idle, life of the Duke and his family, but enchanted with their daughter Lady Corisande to whom he would have proposed had the Duchess permitted it. The Duke and his family are Anglicans. The Cardinal introduces Lothair to the St. Jerome, including their beautiful daughter Clare Arundel who, like Sybil, plans on becoming a nun, because he knows that the intense spiritual life at Vauxe will be more appealing if accompanied by sexual attraction. At Vauxe, Lothair is exposed to the ritual and ceremony of Catholicism as well as to the subtle arguments of the priests, until Grandison arrives to declare that were Lothair to convert he would become the spokesman and defender of 'Divine Truth', and the most important man of the century. But Lothair also becomes acquainted with Theodora who is not only indifferent to religion, but has been the inspiration for the revolutionary Mary Anne societies and is active in revolutionary movements throughout Europe. Phoebus, one member of Theodora's bohemian circle, is a painter and dandy who considers beauty the primary value in life, while regarding books as useless. Lothair is physically attracted to Theodora. At this point, when his loyalties are divided among three women and three district sets of values, he celebrates his coming of age with a lavish party at his Muriel estate, where Corisande helps foil the plot to convert Lothair to Catholicism. However, Theodora wins his loyalty and he vows to devote his life to her. (Lothair's devotion to the person who inspired the Mary Anne societies is a touching tribute that Disraeli pays to his wife, Mary Anne, and to their mutual romantic love which he believed had sustained him throughout his political career.) He goes to Europe and enlists in battle beside Theodora and her colleague General Bruges, in opposition to the forces sponsored by the Pope. In the fight, she is killed and Lothair is seriously wounded. He is nursed to health by Roman Catholics in Rome at the St. Jerome Palace under the direction of Clare Arundel. He agrees to take part in a Catholic service at which she gives thanks for his restored health. But this service proves to be part of a scheme to win him to the Church, for immediately after the service a papal newspaper reports that the Virgin Mary had appeared at the service as a reward for his fighting on behalf of the Pope. Grandison confirms this report and tries to convince Lothair that since he was very ill after he was wounded, he could not be sure for whom he had fought. Then Theodora appears in a vision and admonishes him with the words, 'Lothair, Remember!'; he recalls his commitment to her, and leaves Rome in disgust with Catholic duplicity. He eventually reaches Syria where he meets Paraclete, one of Disraeli's wisdom figures who, after espousing Disraeli's view that God works by races, assures him that despite what the Catholics imply, there is more than one true faith: 'In My Father's house are many mansions' (ch. lxxvii, pp. 411–12). Lothair returns to England, marries Corisande, and embraces the Anglican Church.

Lothair attributes perfection to anything that temporarily fulfils his emotional needs, only to find his original judgment qualified by later experience. Lothair's libido rather than his intellect determines the values he embraces. Passive, lacking in moral energy, and the captive of sincere and well-meaning women who use him (and, in the case of Corisande and Clare Arundel, also allow themselves to be used) in the interests of a religious or political cause, he is hardly an heroic figure. Since Lothair has not established his qualities as a leader or a potential hero, it is hard to see how his marriage to the passive Corisande can possibly signify, as Disraeli may have intended, a change in the direction of England. Lothair's religious quest parallels Tancred's, but the resolution is within the established perimeters of English religious and social life. Unlike Tancred, he returns to English life and is reassimilated into its social fabric. While the novel's conclusion is supposed to represent Lothair's acceptance of the Anglican tradition into which he had been born, it really only shows his continuing attraction to sexually appealing women. Can the reader accept the implication – rather cursorily presented as a *deus ex machina* – that his marriage to Corisande will transform him into an heroic figure? More than most major Victorian novels, *Lothair* shows us how fastidiousness in dealing with sexual matters, whether deriving from the author's sensibility or his sense of his audience's taste, can corrupt both the form and content of a work. If the issues had not been dramatised in terms of sexual attraction, they would have been more sharply defined as well as more plausible. If the women had personalities independent of the values they represented, the basis of their attraction for Lothair would have been more understandable. As it is, Lothair's sexual adolescence and intellectual immaturity intermingle to blur the novel's themes and enervate its major character.

The orphan motif, so pervasive in Disraeli's fiction, shapes the structure of the novel. That Lothair, although belonging to the highest social class, is really an outsider, partly because of the influence of his rigid humourless uncle, engages Disraeli's imagination. Beginning with *Vivian Grey* (1826–7) and *Contarini Fleming* (1832), Disraeli's fiction is often concerned with the influence of childhood on his protagonists' psychic and moral needs. In the opening scenes, it is poignantly ironic that Lothair recollects the Duchess' childhood gift to him, although the gift was such a trifle to her that she had forgotten it. His self-doubt, insecurity, and his need for an early marriage (to confirm his own worth by showing himself that he can attract another person) derive from his peculiar upbringing. That by contrast Corisande and Brentham find sustenance from the love and support of their family is reflected by their poise, confidence and maturity. Lothair is attracted to the families of Vauxe and Brentham because he has a need for the warmth and conviviality that his austere Scottish uncle and the dogmatic and disingenuous Cardinal Grandison do not provide. Brentham and Vauxe seem ideal to him because they combine the nuclear family with social intercourse in an elegant setting. Lothair's premature request for Corisande's hand derives from his desperate need to be loved. Obviously, it is the only socially sanctioned means by which he could become part of the Brentham family. In the early chapters Lothair is more in quest of affection than truth; his desire to marry early is in part a desire to enter into social relationships within a functioning family. He is torn between instinctive loyalty to the Anglican Church and the order and mystery of Catholicism; but more crucially, he is torn between the appeals of Corisande and Clare Arundel and, to a lesser degree, between contending matriarchal claims of the Duchess and Lady St. Jerome.

Later he is attracted to Theodora ostensibly because she seems to be a maternal figure who offers an alternative to the tug of war for his soul, but really because his repressed libido finds her sexually appealing. We cannot doubt that Lothair would willingly have been her lover had she given him the slightest encouragement. For her, he becomes the surrogate for the son that she never had, while for Lothair, she combines the role of surrogate mother and fantasy lover. His pledge to her – whom he addresses at one point as 'adored being' – is the only thing that prevents him from converting to Catholicism (*Lothair*, ch. lix, p. 315). After he is wounded, the Church replaces her in his life and takes him to its breast. Replacing Theodora as a maternal figure, the Catholic clerical structure eases him of his doubt, anxiety and despair after he has lost the apotheosised

Theodora. Disraeli's narrator fully realises that Lothair's spiritual and sexual quests are inextricably interrelated.

While the novel purports to cover two crucial years in Lothair's maturation from an incredible innocent, Lothair does not learn very much. Undoubtedly, the Duchess refuses his request to propose to her daughter because of the folly of his insistence that his views are 'formed on every subject; . . . and, what is more, they will never change' (*Lothair*, ch. v, p. 15). Disraeli ironically uses Phoebus's summary of Lothair – meant by Phoebus as a statement of Lothair's promise – as a telling indictment of Lothair's superficiality: 'You are a good shot, you can ride, you can row, you can swim. That imperfect secretion of the brain which is called thought has not yet bowed your frame. You have not had time to reach much. Give it up altogether' (*Lothair*, ch. lxxvi, p. 402). That Disraeli at 65 felt indulgent to his young hero is indicated by the ambiguous epigraph from Terence, '*Nôsse omnia haec, salus est adolescentulis*' (All this is salvation to a young man).

Disraeli depicts a very amiable young lord with enormous financial resources who is rather lacking in moral and intellectual energy. Does Lothair really develop a programme any more viable than his original determination to eliminate 'pauperism'? Disraeli would have us notice, I think, that Lothair neither achieves spiritual insight, as Tancred had, nor formulates a political programme like Egremont, nor embraces political ideals like Coningsby. In one sense *Lothair* seems to be an effort to clarify, if not rewrite, *Tancred*. But the practical, rational side of Disraeli's dual nature triumphs over his romantic and mystic soul, and the bathetic denouement of *Tancred* is avoided. Lothair's vision of Theodora can be explained on psychological grounds. Under extreme stress, he subconsciously recalls her prior declaration of her immortality which was her *response* when he requested that she reappear if she were to die first (see *Lothair*, ch. xxxiv, p. 179).

The very circularity of form in which Lothair returns to his starting point, Brentham, to claim his original beloved, Corisande, undercuts the idea that he has progressed. No one, including Lothair, appears ready to give the rudderless ship of state real direction. That the aristocrats St. Aldegonde and Brentham are absent from Parliament illustrates that the aristocracy is indifferent to its responsibilities to the people. Life among England's aristocracy is a steady round of social events and foreign travel. Although Lothair has youth, wealth and power, the narrative gradually reveals that the external trappings ensure neither happiness nor opportunity. At times, when the older Disraeli gives way to his delight in grand homes, parties and both secular and religious pageantry, *Lothair* retains vestiges of the Silver Fork tradition with which Disraeli began his career as a novelist. While one does not expect Lothair to experience Gehenna, one wonders whether sybaritic dining might not be at odds with his agonising over his spiritual choices. Disraeli's fascination with the material world of the aristocracy undermines the spirituality of Lothair's quest. In the first part sumptuous dinners at elegant houses are described in such detail that Lothair's crises seem a subsidiary concern.

Once Lothair renounces the voluptuous pleasures of English country houses for service in Theodora's army, Disraeli characteristically moves his narrative into the genre of the picaresque novel where the hero observes the customs of other cultures. That in their last third Disraeli's early novels tended to lurch frantically from place to place may have been a symptom of his inability to sustain his own interest in his characters. But it is a measure of the development of Disraeli's artistry that the major destinations of Lothair's foreign travels do roughly correlate with Lothair's favourite English homes. Vauxe, the centre of Catholicism, anticipates Rome; Belmont anticipates the Greek isle; and the Anglican Brentham home, with which the novel begins and closes, not surprisingly anticipates the Holy Land. Once he departs England, the various places present correlatives to the changing and conflicting demands of Lothair's interior quest. Rome corresponds to his compelling need for order and mystery in religion, the Aegean Isle to his desire to enjoy the pleasure of this world, Syria to his need for the equanimity of complete religious faith, and finally England to his inner need for the moderate but sustaining pleasures of a balanced life with clearly defined responsibilities to self, country and a national Church.

Lothair's intellectual discoveries are hardly what one might expect from 'a nature profound and inquisitive'. In *Lothair*, it is the narrator who plays the role of the wisdom figure until Paraclete is introduced. Worldly and perceptive without being emotional, the narrator understands that Lothair's moments of self-knowledge reveal him as vapid, foolish, hyperbolic and myopic. Disraeli surely would not subscribe to Lothair's juvenile fatalism, when the latter expresses disappointment that he had been unable to establish 'some basis of intimacy' with Theodora on his first visit to Belmont: 'The world seemed dark. . . . However a man may plan his life he is the creature of circumstances. The unforeseen happens and upsets everything. We are mere puppets' (*Lothair*, ch. xxx, p. 140). Lothair's quest involves a sorting out on his part of what is real; he is confronted with religious views, political action, temptations of the senses and mystical experience. He is faced, for example, with the choice of believing either the miracle that is supposed to have occurred to him – no less than the intervention of the Virgin Mary to preserve his life – or the private vision that he experiences. That Lothair's subjective vision of Theodora is at least as real an event as the putative miracle that the Roman Catholic hierarchy manufactures into the event of the century, may be Disraeli's way of making the satirical point that miracles may be either a function of one's desire to believe *or* the church's need to rally its strayed followers.

Disraeli's belief that each man creates his own reality is a marked departure from the political novels in which the protagonists discovered objective truths that the narrators had learned and in which Disraeli believed. Disraeli is very shrewd about how men who debunk religion create their own alternative mysteries. Phoebus apotheosises Theodora as the goddess of his Aryan principles, while Republican ideologues apotheosise her as the spirit of their movement because her picture was on the five-franc piece of the 1850 French Republic. Disraeli is implying that just as Christ has come to mean different things to different people, so the significance and value of a beautiful human can be interpreted by people according to their own psychic needs. By 1870, Disraeli is far more a relativist than in the Young England novels. He is tolerant of the different value systems, and critical not of systems but of duplicity and solipsism. Those are the grounds on which, respectively, Catholicism and Phoebus's paganism are criticised. Yet, while Disraeli is not unsympathetic with Theodora's view that a man's conscience is his church, a view that reflects his own youthful attitude, he now understands the necessity of a national Church as a political institution, because it is desirable for the people of a nation to believe in a controlling deity to which they are morally responsible. The Disraeli of the 1870s also knew the danger of each man acting according to his own conscience. Although Lothair is too submissive and too emotionally captivated to withstand Theodora's influence, he intellectually understands the problem of apotheosising one's conscience: 'Your conscience may be divine . . . and I believe it is; but the consciences of other persons are not divine, and what is to guide them, and what is to prevent or to mitigate the evil they would perpetuate?' (*Lothair*, ch. xxxi, p. 163). The novel dramatises the implications of Lothair's remark; each major position, including the Cardinal's and Phoebus's, shows someone acting on his or her own conscience.

Like most Disraeli novels from *Vivian Grey* through the Young England trilogy, *Lothair* differentiates between an aristocracy of birth and an aristocracy of ability. In contrast to Disraeli, Lothair is born with the highest claims to political position, but really makes no progress in becoming a man of action. On the other hand, General Bruges and Theodora are originally social and political outsiders who, like Beckendorff, Sybil, and even Sidonia, realise their potential through commitment to ideals, whether right or wrong, and through action. Disraeli believed that the antithesis of purposeful and mental physical activity was nullification. If Bruges' life as an adventurer and mercenary seems hardly a suitable example for Lothair, nevertheless there is an integrity about his conduct, about his political negative capability which allows him to participate zealously in the causes to which he commits himself (and to be at least somewhat selective about those causes). His most memorable comment has ironic implications in view of the conclusion, where Lothair is about to be assimilated into the English political and social structure that depends less on ideals than upon compromise and adjustment: 'Action may not always be happiness . . . but there is no happiness without action' (*Lothair*, ch. lxxix, p. 422).

If Theodora represents the alternative of dedication to political ideals, Phoebus illustrates a kind of moral secularism. Disraeli uses him to expose the bankruptcy of erecting one's preference into values and of raising sybaritic behaviour to a theoretical level. Phoebus adopts Theodora's anti-clericalism to his own ends. By having Phoebus extol those who live an instinctive life, Disraeli exposes his Hellenist as a 'strayed reveller'. Phoebus regards the uninhibited celebrations of the natives as religious ceremonies. The inconsistency of Phoebus's ardent anti-religious position is ironically revealed when Phoebus creates his own altar – a statue of Theodora – on the Greek isle. Phoebus is heavily satirised when he abandons Greece to paint the Holy Land at the behest of Russian nobility. This decision hardly seems in keeping with his desires to perpetuate classical ideas and to educate the body at the expense of the mind. Ironically, Phoebus's behaviour contradicts his own definition of virtue: 'the control of the passions, in the sentiment of repose, and the avoidance in all things of excess' (*Lothair*, ch. lxxiii, p. 387). Disraeli implies that something necessary is lost by Phoebus's want of Semitic influence – by which Disraeli means religion and spirituality.

Disraeli means to serve up more than an intellectual smorgasbord in which the reader is exposed to various positions. While the novel tests these doctrines, it discriminates the wheat from the chaff within each. Although it goes to great length to expose Catholic guile, Disraeli still admires the religious intensity of Catholic ceremonies and rituals. While the Anglican Church seems more moderate in its religious commitment and more concerned with this world than the next, it is a national Church which has united England and may continue to do so. It may be a virtue that it does not overwhelm the lives of its devotees and seems to make rather gentle demands upon its followers. It allows even its most devoted followers to love passionately. If Theodora and the Mary-Anne societies ask that one give one's life to its cause, they nevertheless offer solace – no different from that offered by traditional religion – to people to whom the wealthy and powerful, and perhaps the organised churches, do not give their full attention. Their very popularity indicates that, like Chartism in *Sybil*, they are filling a need. If Phoebus's classicism seems immoral, particularly his eugenic programme for propagation of the Aryan race, and if his contention that the love of beauty necessarily leads to virtue seems vague, nevertheless he advocates aesthetic values, if not moral ideals, on which civilisation depends. The appropriately named Paraclete, (a term used for the Holy Spirit and often translated as 'comforter' and 'advocate') is the novel's wisdom figure whom Lothair discovers in Syria; he seems to offer insights towards which the novel has moved. More by his tone, modesty, personal warmth and character than by his words, Paraclete provides an alternative to the pomposity of Phoebus. He does not offer a programme of action for Lothair to adopt and his advice seems rather abstract. It is Lothair who, when looking for validation of his decision not to convert to Catholicism, suggests Paraclete's use of the Anglican distinction between dogma as necessary and Councils which are inessential.

Lothair may have been Disraeli's reaction to *Culture and Anarchy* (1869). Disraeli would have rejected Arnold's association of Hebraism with 'firm obedience' as opposed to 'clear intelligence':

> As Hellenism speaks of thinking clearly, seeing things in their essence and beauty, as a grand and precious feat for man to achieve, so Hebraism speaks of becoming conscious of sin, of awakening to

a sense of sin, . . . To get rid of one's ignorance, to see things as they are, and by seeing them as they are to see them in their beauty, is the simple and attractive ideal which Hellenism holds out before human nature; and from the simplicity and charm of this ideal, Hellenism, and human life in the hands of Hellenism, is invested with a kind of aerial ease, clearness, and radiancy; they are full of what we call sweetness and light.[9]

In contrast, Disraeli had argued in *Lord George Bentinck* not only that Judaism was the source of Christianity's truth, but also that the Hebrew race was the inspiration for the arts in modern Europe, particularly music: 'We hesitate not to say that there is no race at this present, and following in this only the example of a long period, that so much delights, and fascinates, and elevates, and ennobles Europe, as the Jewish'.[10] Disraeli would not have accepted Arnold's cultural archetypes because they directly contradicted his own racial and historical ones. He still believed, as he argued in *Lord George Bentinck*, that Greeks were an exhausted race, while the Jews were the source of both the creative and the moral, both the intellectual and the spiritual.

Arnold's complaint is that religions teach us only to subdue animality, but do not teach, as culture does, the idea of 'human perfection'. Writing of Arnold's concept of culture, Lionel Trilling remarks, 'Culture is not merely a method but an attitude of spirit contrived to receive truth. It is a moral orientation, involving will, imagination, faith: all of these avowedly active elements body forth a universe that contains a truth which the intuition can grasp and the analytic reason can scrutinize'.[11] In response to Arnold's indictment of extant religious institutions, Disraeli proposes the Anglican Church. Arnold argues that British civilisation lacks 'sweetness and light', whereas Disraeli proposes that if aristocrats embrace the Anglican faith, they will make one important step to perfecting the mind and spirit.

Disraeli would not have appreciated the exclusion of politicians from among the ranks of the cultured: 'Now for my part I do not wish to see men of culture asking to be trusted with power'.[12] He would have approved of Arnold's desire for principles of authority, but not of Arnold's questioning whether aristocratic 'wealth, power and consideration are . . . in themselves trying and dangerous things. . . . As to the effect upon the welfare of the community, how can that be salutary, if a class which, by the very possession of wealth, power, and consideration becomes a kind of ideal or standard for the rest of the community, is tried by case and pleasure more than it can well bear, and almost irresistibly carried away from excellence and strenuous virtue?'[13] In fact, Disraeli might have taken Arnold's complaint as a rebuke to himself, his party and his principles.

Disraeli's position is that England depends not on culture, but on the sense of duty of its property holders and the viability of its historical institutions, the Monarchy, Parliament and the Church. Disraeli certainly would not have thought of aristocrats as barbarians; nor would he have thought that the defence of certain traditional principles was a bad thing.

Disraeli would have regarded Arnold's definition of greatness as unworldly and impractical: 'Greatness is a spiritual condition worthy to excite love, interest, admiration; and the outward proof of possessing greatness is that we excite love, interest, and admiration'.[14] For Disraeli greatness consists in being a man of action such as General Bruges or an effective leader of a Parliamentary party. Disraeli is *contending* that the capacity for greatness is a characteristic of personality and temperament and that Lothair has exhibited this characteristic. Yet Disraeli's depiction of Lothair and the great families hardly refutes Arnold's indictment of the aristocracy's parochialism and ennui: 'The care of the Barbarians for the body, and for all manly exercises; the vigour, good looks, and fine complexion which they acquired and perpetuated in their families by these means – all this may be observed still in our aristocratic class. . . . [The aristocratic culture] consisted principally in outward gifts and graces, in looks, manners, accomplishments, prowess'.[15] As we have seen, while Disraeli may imply that Lothair achieves greatness by his marriage and acceptance of Anglicanism, the reader cannot believe that Lothair's superficiality and passivity have permanently disappeared.

III

Endymion is the reflective (and reflexive) creation of an older man who enjoys narrating rather than writing a polemic about England's past. By the time he finished *Endymion*, Disraeli was 75 and had presided over England's destiny for a period of six years from 1874 to 1880. He was no longer the outsider looking in, but the insider looking out. His interest in defining past social forces and political tensions takes a back seat to his interest in demonstrating the fundamentally civilised basis of the English socio-political system. Because the focus is on Endymion's ascent more than the political history of the period from the 1820s through the late 1850s, Disraeli does not confront serious social questions and omits most of the social turmoil in the years covered by *Sybil*, as well as the intellectual issues raised in *Lothair*. His lack of concern for political principles is underlined by his choosing a successful Whig career as his subject, almost as if he wanted to show that he was now above the battle by writing a non-partisan novel with little reference to past or present social issues. In *Endymion*, the views a man holds are far less important than the character of that man. That Endymion is a sympathetic figure as a member of the Whig party which Disraeli spent his political life fighting illustrates the aging statesman's philosophical and political detachment. One hardly expects this from Disraeli unless we realise that in 1880 he saw himself in the role of elder statesman.

Buckle remarks, 'More perhaps than in any other of his novels did [Disraeli] in *Endymion* draw his characters from life'.[16] If one amends his statement to exclude the characters in the early novels who are surrogates for Disraeli, that is surely true. *Endymion* opens in the 1829–30 period. Endymion and Myra are twins of the Ferrars, who have lived beyond their means on the expectation that Mr Ferrars, a Tory, would achieve political prominence. But the Reform Bill blunts his aspirations. Since his financial affairs are in disarray, partly because his late father's estate has been exhausted supporting his son's life-style, the Ferrars are forced to retire to the country and live very modestly. Ferrars is unsuccessful in his efforts to get either an uncontested seat or a position that suits him within Government. His wife's mental and physical health decline. She dies and her husband commits suicide. Thus disappointment and tragedy form the twins' heritage. Myra dedicates herself to Endymion's career, partly out of the desire to restore the family position. Within a rather leisurely plot which emphasises the potential for improving one's condition, Disraeli finds ample room to introduce the Rodneys, who own the lodgings where Endymion dwells; Mrs Rodney's sister Imogene who becomes Lady Beaumaris after she is educated by a young nobleman named Waldershare (based on George Smythe) to become a suitable wife for an Earl; and Mr Vigo, a tailor, who becomes a major holder in railroad stock. At the same lodging house resides Prince Florestan, based on Louis Napoleon, whom Disraeli knew while the former was exiled in England. Myra becomes a companion and close friend of Adrianna Neuchatel (a family based on the British Rothschilds). That relationship gives her the opportunity to meet and marry Lord Roehampton (based on Lord Palmerston, England's Foreign Secretary). But one motive for her marriage is that she sees it as a way of aiding her brother's career. At this point, Endymion's career begins to progress rapidly. He becomes secretary to a Cabinet minister, Sidney Wilton, who had once been his father's friend and rival and finds an important sponsor in Lady Montfort who is estranged from her idiosyncratic husband and who adopts Endymion as her protégé. Because of his lack of means, Endymion is reluctant to run for Parliament, but he receives an anonymous £20,000 which he learns much later is a gift of Adrianna Neuchatel. Upon his election in 1841 he becomes secretary and spokesman for Lord Roehampton. when Lord Montfort dies, he marries Lady Montfort, and his widowed sister marries Florestan. As the novel closes Endymion becomes Prime Minister.

While Endymion parallels *Coningsby* as a *Bildungsroman* about the growth of a political leader, Endymion's character is less affected by the political and historical events whirling around him than by family and intimate friends. Like Coningsby, Endymion is exposed to a number of positive and negative examples and he must choose among them. Lord Montfort replaces Monmouth as the solipsistic alternative that must be rejected. If there is no conceptual guide to parallel Sidonia, it is because Disraeli is implicitly emphasising the practical rather than the theoretical. Mostly by example rather than by articulated philosophy, the idealistic, iconoclastic Lord Roehampton and the pragmatic Sidney Wilton shape his political education. But women are the major influences upon Endymion, undoubtedly because Disraeli felt in his later years that Mrs Austen, his sister Sarah, his wife Mary Anne, Lady Blessington, Lady Bradford and even the Queen had played crucial roles in his career. While Levine maintains that the 'fates of the central figures are at least partially shaped by politics', one could argue, on the contrary, politics are virtually irrelevant.[17] Despite the recurrence of Tadpole and Taper from *Sybil*, actual historical events which are mentioned remain apart from the dramatic action as if Disraeli's imagination could no longer use historical material to adumbrate character. The factual source material forms a penumbra that is never synthesised into the novel's structure and theme. Nor does Endymion have a political philosophy. Is the political history in the novel really any more than a superficial recording of the changes of governments? Whether intended or not, the novel's cumulative implication is the inanity of such changes.

The romance of Endymion regaining the family position appealed to Disraeli, who, as we have seen, believed that he himself belonged to a family and a race which was more than the equal of the English nobility and that he was a kind of paradigm illustrating that England was a land of opportunity. In this last novel, Disraeli is more intrigued by the process by which power is obtained than by the goals of power. Endymion's ascent rather than the quality of his mind or his capacity for leadership is the subject. Because people are always doing things for him, he lacks the energy, ambition and dash of the typical Disraeli hero. Looking back with delight upon his own ascent, despite his position as an outsider and despite his having been patronised as an eccentric and a dandy, Disraeli dramatises the social and political ascent of a host of characters who, by a combination of strong will and good luck, overcome personal and family adversity. The most prominent illustrations are Endymion and Myra who suffered their father's loss of fortune and suicide and their mother's madness and premature death. Upward mobility is an important concept in *Endymion*. Both the Rodneys as well as Mr Vigo and Imogene Beaumaris emerge from the middle class, while Nigel Penruddock and Job Thornberry emerge from obscure country families to become significant factors in the nation's religious and political life. Penruddock is a cleric who eventually converts to Roman Catholicism and finally becomes an Archbishop and Papal legate to England. Thornberry is the son of a farmer who becomes a mill-owner, a leader of the Anti-Corn League and a Radical. But in later years he becomes a country gentleman and, although a 'respected member of the Cabinet', no longer represents the views of most of his constituents. Perhaps the irrelevance of ideology is best illustrated by Thornberry who at first espouses Free Trade and the interests of those not owning land, but then gradually settles into the life of a country gentleman and is addressed as 'squire'.

The narrator defines by example the virtues of tolerance, tact and intelligence that he values. The novelist within the novel, St. Barbe, provides an insensitive and amoral antitype to the kind of novelist that Disraeli wishes to be. His solipsism, his envy of the accomplishments and good fortune of others, and his willingness to misconstrue deliberately his journalistic account of an event for his own purposes, are contrasted with the speaker's good nature and benevolence. Whether he is, as I suspect, a caricature of Thackeray or, as has been suggested, of Carlyle, or both, St. Barbe functions within the novel as the kind of journalist and historian who deserves scorn because he myopically perceives the pattern of events he observes and regards all men as a mirror image of his solipsistic, conniving self.[18]

Endymion is about the art – the choreography, the tempo, the style and the technique – of creating a career and Disraeli's narrator is a pervasive and anxious presence as the director of this performance. The essential lack of creativity, imagination and passion on the part of the title character is in striking contrast to the inventiveness of the speaker's mind. In his late novels Disraeli is fascinated with those who have the imaginative resources to posit a putative identity and the energy and will to embrace it. Examples are to be found not only in the protagonists but also in the secondary cast: Myra, Theodora, Phoebus, the Rodneys and Imogene Beaumaris.

The opening sets the stage for Endymion's father's tragic demise. Filled with false prophecy (Ferrars will be Prime Minister; Ferrars will be in Parliament before he is 40), expectations are raised only to be abruptly crushed. Because of the opening, the reader finds himself wondering after Endymion's star begins to rise whether the novel's structure is to be iterative and cyclic or whether Endymion will mark a new turn in the family chronicle. Myra's aspiring parents are economically and psychologically destroyed by a reversal of personal and economic fortune. The twins do not quite put behind them their memories of their parents' sudden reversal of fortune and subsequent madness and suicide. No matter how their aspirations seem to be progressing, the twins irrationally and even subconsciously fear the imminent collapse of their fortunes. Mrs Ferrars' infantile regression takes Disraeli into the darker recesses of the human psyche. Disraeli renders her collapse in terms of an Ophelia-like distraction, marked by confusion between essentials and trivia, between central issues and peripheral effects: 'After all, the poor King of France is much worse off than we are. However, I cannot now buy the Duchess of Sevres' lace, which I had promised her to do. It is rather awkward. However, the best way always is to speak the truth. I must tell the Duchess I am powerless, and that we are the victims of a revolution, like herself' (*Endymion*, ix, p. 40). Her perception of herself as a member of the *ancien régime*; her lack of logic and her irrationality; and her retreat into an autistic world show Disraeli's understanding that women who depend on men to define them are vulnerable to collapse. That Myra, his twin sister, replaces Endymion's mother in the role of ambitious but protective parent reflects Disraeli's closeness and gratitude to his sister Sarah who seems to have partially replaced in his psyche his mother, whom he regarded as a weak, ineffectual figure. Yet one wonders whether Disraeli subconsciously needed to exorcise guilt that he felt for disrupting the family paradigm by displacing his mother with his sister. In contrast to her mother's hollowness and passivity, Myra's goal of reversing the family disgrace and the means by which she fulfils that goal make her the novel's most dynamic character. While the narrator, Disraeli's surrogate, often patronises Endymion as he carefully and judiciously ascends the political ladder, he is in awe of Myra's and, to a lesser extent, Lady Montfort's *Realpolitik*. Whether Disraeli intended it or not, there is a darker side to Myra's dedication to Endymion. Within her burns Disraeli's own fiery ambition and his continuing desire to show how by force of will a person can triumph over those who would patronise, ignore or deliberately exclude him. Myra is unscrupulous, recognising no morality except her commitment to her brother. She is obsessed with the idea of advancement for Endymion and, lest the family tragedy should repeat itself, with economic independence. Arranging her marriages according to the advantage it will afford her and trying to do the same for her brother, Myra is a Machiavelli of the boudoir. Had not Myra married Lord Roehampton even more for the advantage it would bring Endymion than for love? Later, her attraction to Florestan derives at first from his having befriended Endymion. Myra must repress and direct her passionate love for Endymion into socially sanctioned behaviour. Because of her constant fear that her success will be reversed by a change in circumstances, she requires positional assurance even more than money. Speare's view that 'her acts . . . [lack] real cohesion and consistency, so that some of the exhibitions of her character seem accidental and even meaningless' does a disservice to one of Disraeli's most subtle and complex character studies.[19]

Myra, an evolution of the title character's sister Miriam in *Alroy*, is Endymion's double. Myra more intensely feels the passions and emotions that relate to the family disgrace, resurrection and triumph. It is she who experiences the humiliation, the fanatical need to restore the family honour, the anxiety lest Endymion fail to make a marriage that establishes his position. She is the libidinous, passionate and emotional part of Endymion. Even before her mother's madness and her father's suicide, she perceives the family's plight in exaggerated and hysterical terms. While Endymion accepts his change of circumstances, she feels 'as if we had fallen from some star' (*Endymion*, ch. xi, p. 45). When she refuses Nigel's proposal, she does not at first declare to whom she has committed herself as if she somehow senses the psycho-sexual overtones of her intense avowal. But when he inquires, she acknowledges her secret life:

> 'My life is devoted to Endymion. There is a mystic bond between us, originating, perhaps, in the circumstances of our birth; for we are twins. . . . I shall be in the world, whatever be my lot, high or low – the active, stirring world – working for him, thinking only of him. Yes; moulding events and circumstances in his favour', and she spoke with fiery animation, 'I have brought myself, by long meditation, to the conviction that a human being with a settled purpose must accomplish it, and that nothing can resist a will that will stake even existence for its fulfillment.' (*Endymion*, ch. xxvi, p. 118)

Myra requires the fiction of a 'mystic bond'. Part of her passionate commitment to her brother derives from her subconscious desire to triumph over the situation that destroyed not only her father but herself. She knows that she as a woman cannot be the means of reviving family honour. Myra's dominance of her brother, along with the narrator's tone, contributes to the condescension with which the reader regards Endymion.

Disraeli felt that men of distinction required the support of women. At every stage of his career he felt the presence of a strong female figure – his sister Sarah, Mrs Austen, his wife and Lady Bradford. But he did not conceive the female in the background as the traditional Victorian figure who comforts her male. Disraeli believed in the power of refined woman to cultivate and soften the aggressive impulses of men into socially acceptable channels. The acquaintance of 'refined and charming women . . . refines the taste, quickens the perception, and gives, as it were, a grace and flexibility to the intellect' (*Coningsby*; V, i, p. 257). Disraeli's attitude to women should not be confused with Victorian women worship. The 1978 exhibition at the Royal Academy, London entitled *Great Victorian Pictures* enables us to understand how innovative are Disraeli's depictions of women. In Myra and Theodora he rejects the self-absorbed women whom we see in the paintings of Marcus Stone, William Edward Frost and George Adolphus Storey. Nor does Disraeli perceive womanhood as a sacrament. In his novels, forceful, creative women can have immeasurable effect upon the world. Women can take the initiative in loving, marrying and directing politics. Certainly, Disraeli never would have written, like George Eliot, 'A loving woman's world lies within the four walls of her own home, and it is only through her husband that she is in any electric communication with the world beyond' ('Amos Barton', *Scenes of Clerical Life*, I, ch. 7).

Disraeli's women have vigorous independent minds and act on their own. Often they have an emotional range and sensibility that men lack. As the novels progress women become increasingly important. They provide the title figures of the novels of the mid-1830s, and in *Sybil* the title character is a major source of the novel's humane values; she represents the people's potential to renew themselves. In *Sybil* and the last three novels, the social world that is dominated by women seems to be as important as Parliamentary debate in shaping events. In the last novels women become the most energetic characters; not only Myra, but Theodora and Lady Montfort are figures of passion and courage. Disraeli's women may lack the blatant sexuality of contemporary women, but he was writing within conventions that limited his possibilities. Disraeli does not assign women to domestic roles or make them idle self-indulgent figures within a masculine world. Compared to Esther in *Bleak House*, Estella in *Great Expectations*, or Little Dorritt, many of Disraeli's women are not only vibrant personalities, but often aggressive and bold. More than his peers, Disraeli recognises the energy and passion of women.

Disraeli the novelist was divided between his own rather latitudinarian impulses towards sex and the knowledge that he must not offend Victorian scruples if he were to fulfil his ambition. After all, he had a scandalous affair with Henrietta Sykes which he never really regretted, as well as a prior affair with Mrs Clara Bolton. Disraeli enjoys writing about those who were not always bound by Victorian sexual mores. In *Coningsby*, he goes out of his way to include the antics of Lord Monmouth (Lord Hertford) who lives with his bastard child by a French actress, marries the step-daughter of his mistress, and enjoys the company of promiscuous women. And he wrote about Byron's unconventional behaviour in *Venetia*.

Disraeli wanted to show that the movement from obscurity to prominence – the movement that mimed his own career – could be accomplished without guile or excessive ambition. To accomplish this, he transfers the morally ambiguous activity necessary to climb the greasy pole to Myra and, to an extent, Lady Montfort, a woman who for a time uses him rather as a plaything to compensate for her own failed marriage, and whom he finally marries when she is widowed. The latter, too, is a divided personality. Because of the frustrations of her apparently asexual marriage to a man who ignores her, Lady Montfort funnels her sublimated passionate energy into political machinations that aid Endymion's career. The intensity, determination and ruthlessness of Lady Montfort and Myra undermine Endymion's stature within the novel. When he becomes Prime Minister, one can be excused for remarking that Endymion is a man lacking in real intellectual ability whose fate is controlled by his sister and Lady Montfort. In contrast to the activities of Myra, Lady Montfort and Adriana Neuchatel on his behalf, his memories of his parents' demise virtually paralyse Endymion with fears of his own political downfall. During the medieval tournament, Endymion falls into a period of despair when he even contemplates suicide because he feels that he is being ignored: 'Endymion felt all that embarrassment, mingled with a certain portion of self-contempt, which attends the conviction that we are what is delicately called *de trop* (*Endymion*, ch. lx, p. 269). That the narrative voice uses the collective pronoun is revealing. Disraeli's urgency and empathy for Endymion's sense of exclusion hint that even after great success his own fear of being the outsider has never been purged. Disraeli's voice identifies with those who have suffered undeserved social rebuke.

Finally, *Endymion* is a bourgeois novel about succeeding in an aristocratic world. In *Endymion*, Disraeli's satire is more social than political; his target is the aristocracy's façade, hypocrisy, and moral sloth. Commitments based on family and personal ties are far more enduring than social relationships that are exposed as no more than steps in an elaborate dance. Illustrative of his good-natured social satire is his description of Zenobia:

> Zenobia was the queen of London, of fashion, and of the Tory Party. When she was not holding high festivals, or attending them, she was always at home to her intimates, and as she deigned but rarely to honour the assembly of others with her presence, she was generally at her evening post to receive the initiated. To be her invited guest under such circumstances proved at once that you had entered the highest circle of the social Paradise. (*Endymion*, ch. ii, p. 5)

Disraeli directs his irony at those whose lives are façades and to whom paradise is being in the presence of a snob whose favour has little to do with merit. Indeed, the language implies that traditional religion has been replaced by social rituals with their own 'high festivals' for their 'initiates' and their own definition of what constitutes 'paradise', namely to be in the presence of the social goddess. Disraeli's fascination with wealth and power extends to the new breed of aristocrat produced by bold, shrewd investments. While he appreciates the energy and drive that have made possible trains and postal service, and has given *élan* to London, at the same time he is somewhat concerned that these people have lost touch with the past political and religious principles that had sustained England. The epitome of the successful city men who financed the technological advances of the Victorian period, Mr Neuchatel finances the Liberals in part out of class resentment against the nobility rather than out of political conviction: 'So you are a little frightened. . . . Well; we City men must see what we can do against the dukes. You may put me down for double his amount' (*Endymion*, ch. xxx, p. 132). Yet Disraeli as a septuagenarian cannot help but sympathise with Neuchatel's desire to undermine the complacency of the ancient aristocracy and his optimism that enables one to live almost hubristically, as if the present were perpetual; Neuchatel brings the kind of self-confidence, will and energy to his business that Disraeli had brought to politics.

In *Endymion*, Disraeli is not sure whether he wants to endorse ambition and the will to power, or play the role of an elder statesman who is above the battle. But as the novel progresses his narrator seems to become more committed to the energetic pursuit of power for its own sake. While Florestan, the man who believes with apocalyptic certainty that he is one of the elect whose fate it is to rule, is at first regarded with some irony, Endymion's characteristic caution is patronised. Although Disraeli depicts Florestan as a rather unscrupulous opportunist whose arrogant belief in his destiny allows him to believe the ends justify the means, the ultimate *success* of his programme in large measure finally exonerates him in Disraeli's eyes. Thus *Realpolitik* itself becomes a value. Nor should this surprise us in the man whom Asa Briggs speaks of as practising 'a Toryism of imaginative opportunism rather than principle, an opportunism that mystified and shocked'.[20] Rather more kindly, Gertrude Himmelfarb argues: 'What has commonly been understood as Disraeli's opportunism may be accurately rendered as latitudinarianism. And latitudinarianism is as respectable a doctrine in politics as it is in theology.'[21] In any case, the aesthetic quality of the novel is enhanced by Disraeli's ambiguity, because it creates a rather complex vision of characters who continually threaten to become oversimplified. Both Endymion and Florestan have been dispossessed by circumstances for which they are not responsible, but while Florestan is responsible for his own return to power, Endymion depends upon the manipulation of others. In Disraeli's later novels, the quality of a man counts far more than his programme. But if Florestan represents a more Romantic younger self that Disraeli never completely suppresses, Sidney Wilton speaks for the more cautious and pragmatic older self that Disraeli has created when he responds to Florestan: 'I really do not understand what destiny means. . . . I understand what conduct means, and I recognize that it should be regulated by truth and honour. I think a man had better have nothing to do with destiny, particularly if it is to make him forfeit his parole' (*Endymion*, ch. xli, pp. 180–1). On one hand, Disraeli admires Florestan's boldness, practicality and force of will; on the other, he insists upon the decorum, dignity and modesty exemplified by the character of Wilton. Yet he knew that his own career and that of any outsider depended more on energy than decorum, and that Endymion had the luxury of Myra and Lady Montfort who acted boldly on his behalf. And he shows that at times Endymion, while taking an expedient course, deludes himself as to motive and clothes his ambition in ideals.

IV

We recall that Disraeli, like Carlyle, felt that English people required bold and imaginative leaders to capture their imaginations and to stir them to discover what Arnold called their better selves. The real leader is one who knows how to deal with his fellows from careful observation and who has the welfare of the nation uppermost in his mind. For Disraeli the necessary qualities of leadership are perseverance, tact, energy and self-control. Yet Disraeli is ambivalent about the heroic possibilities of both Lothair and Endymion and their abilities to bridge political and social divisions. Neither Endymion nor Lothair really answers the mournful complaint voiced by Disraeli's Tancred in 1847:

> No one has confidence in himself; on the contrary, everyone has a mean idea of his own strength and no reliance on his judgment. Men obey a general impulse, they bow before an external

necessity, whether for resistance or action. Individuality is dead; there is a want of inward and personal energy in man; and that is what people feel and mean when they go about complaining there is no faith. (*Tancred*, Bk. II, ch. xiv, p. 147)

If we begin to understand how and why these putative heroic figures fail, we may come closer to understanding Disraeli's final novels. At times Disraeli is sympathetic to the protagonists even while he is satirising them as lacking in will or energy. Although he condescends to them, he sympathises with their hopes and aspirations, and with their quest for a stable nuclear family. At first they seem the younger selves he would have liked to have been, living comfortably within an elegant aristocratic world. But Lothair is an orphan, and Endymion never quite recovers from losing the family equilibrium and security after his father's fortunes decline and his mother begins to go mad. Rather pathetically, Lothair says 'I wish I were a hero'; he is not heroic because his mind, as he recognises, is 'uncertain and unsettled' (*Lothair*, ch. xxxi, pp. 160–1). Endymion, too, wants to 'step out of the crowd' and possess 'power', but he does not convince the reader that he would know how to use it (*Endymion*, ch. xxxvi, p. 155–6).

After *Sybil* (1845), the second novel of the trilogy, Disraeli's major characters really do not discover essential principles with which to lead the community, but rather search for something beyond politics to compensate for a lack they feel within themselves. Tancred seeks religious truth; Lothair seeks both religion and another person who will fulfil him; Endymion seeks personal relationships. Unlike Tancred or Alroy, Lothair has no religious awakening; unlike Coningsby or Egremont, Endymion does not discover political principles. In these novels, particularly *Endymion*, pliability and flexibility become values in themselves: a man must learn how to make the political and social structure work for himself. In the political trilogy, men had the opportunity to shape history; in these novels, history (the concatenation of circumstances in which a man lives) shapes men. Rather than present relentless judgment of a social system that desperately needs changing as in *Sybil*, Disraeli's last novels perceive the social and political order as a benign self-regulating system which corrects its own errors and which is fundamentally untouched by hypocrisy, sloth and vindictiveness. In *Lothair* and *Endymion*, despite St. Barbe's envy and spite, despite the Cardinal's massive duplicity, despite Fenian rallies and European revolution, England's essential health survives.

Conclusion

Disraeli's ultimate aesthetic triumph was his political career. Before he was elected to Parliament, he spoke of the day when he would become Prime Minister. His career was predicated on his ability to imagine himself in a position and then to find the resources to attain that position. By position, I mean not only a post but a political attitude, stance or policy. Disraeli instinctively adopted the role necessary to further his political career. As Robert Blake has remarked, 'He knew that he had to preserve an iron control over his voice and countenance if he was to avoid revealing the passion and ambition which seethed in his mind. Hence his assumption of that magniloquent half-ironic half-serious manner which so disconcerted those who had expected the ordinary self-deprecatory candour of the English upper class.'[1]

Disraeli's career tells us something about the continuities between life and art. Disraeli used his novels not only to create the political figure he became but also to define his essential character and personality. His first six novels – *Vivian Grey*, *The Young Duke*, *Contarini Fleming*, *Alroy*, *Henrietta Temple*, *Venetia* – were outlets for his fantasies, fears, hopes and doubts. The novels provided him with the sense that he could impose an order on the recalcitrant flow of events. Were it not for his first six novels – his romances about young heroes – written prior to his election to Parliament, he would not have discovered the self he wanted to be. Indulging his fantasy in heroic exploits and passionate love affairs provided a necessary outlet for his frustrated energies. Moreover, he objectified in his protagonists parts of himself that he wanted to exorcise, while creating in his more mature narrator the balance, judgment and character he required to fulfil his political and social ambitions. The early novels compensated for the disappointment at not achieving prominence. In the late 1820s and 1830s, he felt that, although he had aristocratic blood and deserved to be esteemed on the grounds of birth as well as merit, his heritage and accomplishments were patronised. Dandyism was another kind of self-dramatisation for Disraeli; it fulfilled his need for public attention at the same time as it enabled him to show himself that he was unique. His arrogance, self-assertiveness and flamboyance made him unpopular; yet his novels and his behaviour show that he needed to have love and companionship. When Disraeli created characters within fiction, he created, tested and often discarded tentative models for the various selves which he brought to the disparate social and private roles he was called upon to play.

Disraeli's compulsion for self-dramatisation, extravagance and hyperbole finds an outlet in his political career. When, after he was first elected to Parliament in 1837, he required a forum to articulate his social, political and spiritual principles, he returned to fiction and wrote the Young England trilogy – *Coningsby* (1844), *Sybil* (1845) and *Tancred* (1847). The trilogy was a testing ground for his political and moral philosophy. Young England itself was another of Disraeli's fictions and, like his novels, enabled him to voice extravagant aspects of his complex and often contradictory political views. As the climax to the trilogy, *Tancred* emphasises the need to discover faith and mystery as the bases for political health and proposes a theocracy as the way to reunite man with God and to make government 'again divine'. But *Tancred* is a fairy tale; even in the trilogy, except for most of *Sybil*, Disraeli is still using his novels as escapes from the frustrating world of responsibilities.

When he actually achieved power, he ignored the romantic, visionary nostalgic tenets of Young England. While in office he was conservative but practical and did not oppose reasonable compromise. John Manners may have understood the tentative nature of Disraeli's beliefs when he wrote of Disraeli in his journal: 'His historical views are quite mine, but does he believe them?'[2] Disraeli tested an idea or an attitude by committing himself to it fully, by making it his own and living it. This, much more than expedience and hypocrisy, explains his notable political flip-flop on the Corn Laws or his change from Radical to Tory. Disraeli changed his attitudes in response to his experience, as when he condemned Catholicism in *Lothair*, because he felt the church had become a divisive force in English life. Disraeli published no fiction for twenty-three years between *Tancred* and *Lothair* because his imagination and creativity found an outlet in politics. He wrote *Lothair* and more than half of *Endymion* while he was out of office from 1868–74, and completed *Endymion* after his second term as Prime Minister. Even in these final novels, his personality looms as larger than life. Just as he created a splendid public figure who lived a fantastic career, he created in all his novels characters who often play roles, adopt disguises, and undergo radical transformations of status and personality. His novels, like his public career, are about the *art* of creating life.

Disraeli's career as a novelist shows a movement toward increased sophistication. In his early novels – *Vivian Grey*, *The Young Duke*, *Contarini Fleming*, and *Alroy* – Disraeli uses himself as the principal subject. Since the novels dramatise his experiences, ideas, attitudes and feelings, our appreciation of their aesthetic value depends in part upon knowing something about young Disraeli. The form of the novels depends upon a tension between the exuberant, energetic, bold and independent title character, and the mature, controlled speaker who is often an older version of the hero. Both characters are versions of Disraeli. In *Henrietta Temple* and *Venetia*, Disraeli moves from self-immersion to reflection and creates characters who are more independent of his psyche. Not only do his plots become more organised, but as the historical sweep of the opening chapters of *Henrietta Temple* shows, he begins to see the potential for enlarging the scope of his imagined world and miming the factual world. As Disraeli's career as a novelist progresses, his plots become more disciplined and tightly organised. He no longer indulges in delightful but digressive Shandean flights and is less likely to allow the discrete epigram to take precedence over the process of presenting the imagined world of the novel. He learned to use his novels to argue his political and philosophical points of view. In *Coningsby* and *Sybil*, he organised his plots into a coherent theory of economic and historical cause and effect, and created characters not only as unique human beings but as representatives of social and political events. (These novels pointed the way for the inclusion of political and social issues in the novels of Trollope and Dickens.) If, in the Young England trilogy, Disraeli discovered that the novel could be used to urge political, historical and religious ideas, in *Lothair* he used it to explore major Victorian world views. In *Lothair* and *Endymion*, he shows his increasing interest in subconscious motives, obsessions and fixations.

Disraeli deserves to be read and reread. His early novels not only move us by the protagonists' intense quests for values, but by their teeming life, their exuberance, and their understanding of the ambitious, idealistic, heroic figures. The later novels give us a panoramic vision of Victorian life from the unique perspective of a man who sat in Parliament and held high office. In all his novels Disraeli was an astute observer of manners and morals. Reading his novels gives a sense of the changing mores of nineteenth-century social and political life from 1826–80. From what other novelist do we learn so much about the Oxford Movement, the position of Catholics in England, and the human consequences of bad harvests and exploitative landlords?

While we read Disraeli to supplement our view of the nineteenth century, we also read Disraeli because he is a splendid artist. His cosmopolitan, lively, often ironic voice engages our attention whether he is presenting the aspirations of potential heroes or the failures of political and religious institutions. The sheer joy in telling is Disraeli's most marvellous asset and delights the reader even if the plot wobbles as it does on occasion, particularly in the early *Vivian Grey* and *The Young Duke*. He was a brilliant satirist throughout his career as the caricatures of St. Barbe and Von Aslingen demonstrate. Disraeli knew how to select carefully and how to exaggerate details in order to transform a character into a grotesque, but he also knew how to develop a character meticulously by showing him or her in diverse situations. Disraeli is a profound psychologist, and his understanding of human behaviour becomes more and more complex and subtle. The infinite variety of his novels reflects his exuberant enjoyment of the variety he found in life. His great dramatic scenes – the Young Duke in his gambling den, Ferdinand in the sponging-house, Sybil's search for her father through London, The Diggs's tommy shop – remain with us together with the other great moments in English fiction.

Notes

Introduction

1. Levine's book was completed although not published before Robert Blake's monumental *Disraeli* (London: Eyre and Spottiswoode, 1966). He thus does not take account of Blake's work. See Levine, p. 9.
2. A. B. Walkley, *The Times*, 5 July 1922, p. 12; quoted in R. W. Stewart, *Disraeli's Novels Reviewed, 1826–1968* (Metuchen, N. J.: The Scarecrow Press, 1975), p. 160.
3. Lord David Cecil, *Early Victorian Novels* (London: Constable, 1934), p. 290n.
4. John Holloway, *The Victorian Sage* (New York: Macmillan, 1953), p. 107.
5. Sir Isaiah Berlin, 'Benjamin Disraeli, Karl Marx, and the Search for Identity', *Transactions of the Jewish Historical Society*, 22 (1968–9), p. 8.

Chapter 1. Metaphors of the Self: Disraeli's Early Fiction

1. Thomas Mann, *A Sketch of My Life*, trans. H. T. Lowe-Porter, 1930, 1st American edn (New York: Knopf, 1960), pp. 43–4.
2. 'Mutilated Diary', Hughenden Papers, A/III/C. Others who have commented on this crucial entry include: Robert Blake, *Disraeli* (London: Eyre & Spottiswoode, 1966); B. R. Jerman, *The Young Disraeli* (Princeton, New Jersey: Princeton University Press, 1960); William F. Monypenny and George E. Buckle, *The Life of Benjamin Disraeli, Earl of Beaconsfield*, 6 vols. (London: John Murray, 1910–20).
3. See Blake, 27–33.
4. Page references throughout the text refer to the readily accessible Hughenden Edition (London: Longmans & Green & Co., 1882). Book (or Part) and chapter number, indicated respectively by upper and lower case Roman numerals are standard for every edition. My source for the original edition of *Vivian Grey* and *The Young Duke* is the less accessible but authoritative Centenary Edition, ed. Lucian Wolf (London: Alexander Moring, Ltd., 1904–5). Unfortunately only two volumes ever appeared in this edition.
5. Quoted by Blake, p. 93.
6. Jerman, p. 37.
7. See Wolf, Introduction to *Vivian Grey*, The Centenary Edition, p. xxxviii.
8. Blake, p. 37.
9. Jerman, p. 50.
10. See *The Merry Wives of Windsor*, II, ii, 2–3. Pistol defiantly speaks these lines when Falstaff refuses to lend him money.
11. See Jerman, pp. 92–5.
12. Wolf, Introduction to *The Young Duke*, The Centenary Edition, pp. xiii–xiv.
13. Wolf, Introduction to *The Young Duke*, The Centenary Edition, p. xviii. Blake,

however, contends that Wolf does not support this argument, p. 56.

14. See Disraeli's *Vindication of the English Constitution* (1835) and Chapter 3 of *Sybil* (1845).
15. Quoted in Asa Briggs, *Victorian People: A Reassessment of Persons and Themes, 1851–67* (Chicago: The University of Chicago Press, 1955), p. 278.
16. Quoted in Briggs, p. 282.
17. See Blake, pp. 297–300.
18. Jerman, p. 136.
19. T. S. Eliot, 'Hamlet', *Selected Essays*, revised edn (New York: Harcourt Brace, and World, 1960), pp. 124–5.
20. Blake, p. 77.
21. See Monypenny and Buckle, I, 176.
22. *Encyclopedia Judaica* (New York: Macmillan, 1971), I, pp. 750–1.
23. Quoted in Monypenny and Buckle, I, 194.
24. Quoted in Stephen R. Graubard, *Burke, Disraeli and Churchill* (Cambridge: Harvard University Press, 1961); p. 139.
25. See Chapter xxiv entitled 'The Jewish Question' in *Lord George Bentinck* (London: Archibald Constable and Company, 1905), pp. 314–30.
26. Quoted in Monypenny and Buckle, I, p. 198.
27. *Encyclopedia Judaica*, X, p. 490; I, 750.
28. Martin Price, 'The Other Self: Thoughts About Character in the Novel', in *Imagined Worlds*, eds Maynard Mack and Ian Gregor (London: Methuen & Co., 1968), p. 280.
29. Harold Fisch, 'Disraeli's Hebraic Compulsions', in *Essays Presented to Chief Rabbi Israel Brodie on the Occasion of His Seventieth Birthday*, eds H. S. Zimmels, J. Rabbinowitz and I. Finestein (London: The Soncino Press, 1967), p. 91.
30. M. H. Abrams, 'English Romanticism: The Spirit of the Age', in *Romanticism and Consciousness*, ed. Harold Bloom (New York: Norton, 1970), pp. 102–3.

Chapter 2. From Immersion to Reflection: Romance and Realism in 'Henrietta Temple' and 'Venetia'

1. Richard A. Levine, *Benjamin Disraeli* (New York: Twayne, 1968), p. 58.
2. Walter E. Houghton, *The Victorian Frame of Mind* (New Haven: Yale University Press, 1957), p. 392.
3. Blake, p. 16; see also p. 154.
4. Quoted in James Ogden, *Isaac D'Israeli* (Oxford: The Clarendon Press, 1969), p. 190.
5. See Jerman for an account of Disraeli's relationship with the Austens and Henrietta Sykes, especially Chapters 6 to 8.
6. While the original edition has a slightly more exuberant voice and an occasionally more effusive and silly Henrietta, Blake's implication that it has been bowdlerised in a manner similar to *Vivian Grey* and *The Young Duke* is somewhat misleading. See Blake, p. 37n.
7. Leslie Stephen, *Hours in a Library*, Vol. II (London: Smith, Eldes & Co., 1892), p. 108.
8. Jerman, p. 286; see Blake, p. 422.
9. 'The Mutilated Diary', Hughenden Papers, A /III /C. See Jerman, p. 190, for the entire passage.

10. See Blake, pp. 150–65.
11. 'The Mutilated Diary', Hughenden Papers, A/III/C. See Blake, pp. 136–40.
12. Jerman, p. 277; but I disagree with Jerman's contention that 'Ferdinand Armine in nowise resembles Benjamin Disraeli'.
13. Blake, p. 48.
14. Blake, p. 144.
15. Monypenny and Buckle, I, p. 342.
16. The novel was originally entitled *Venetia or the Poet's Daughter*; for more on the Byron and Shelley parallel, see Monypenny and Buckle, I, pp. 360–4.
17. After several tries, he was elected in 1837.
18. Blake, p. 288.
19. Quoted in Monypenny and Buckle, I, p. 338.
20. With characteristic immodesty, he speaks of the 'artists's' difficulty in using such a style: '[This] style . . . is a delicate and difficult instrument for an artist to handle. . . . He must alike beware the turgid and the bombastic, the meagre and the mean. He must be easy in his robes of state, and a degree of elegance and dignity must accompany him even in the camp and the market house. The language must rise gradually with the rising passions of the speakers and subside in harmonious unison with their sinking emotions'. Quoted in Monypenny and Buckle, I, p. 198. This preface was omitted in later editions.
21. *Shelley*, ed. A. S. B. Glover (London: The Nonesuch Press, 1951), p. 1030.
22. Nevertheless, Disraeli probably appreciated the review of *Henrietta Temple* in the *New Monthly Magazine* which observed: 'In any other age than the present, or even now, had he lived less in society, Mr. Disraeli would have been a poet. He has essentially the poetic temperament – the intense self-consciousness, the impetuosity, and the eye for the beautiful'. Quoted in R. W. Stewart, *Disraeli's Novels Reviewed, 1836–* 1968 (Metuchen, N. J.: The Scarecrow Press, 1975), p. 155.
23. He would certainly have insisted on the inclusion of novelists in the following statement that Shelley made of poets in *A Defence of Poetry*: 'For he not only beholds intensely the present as it is, and discovers those laws according to which present things ought to be ordered, but he beholds the future in the present, and his thoughts are the germs of the flower and the fruit of latest time'. *Shelley*, pp. 1026–7.

Chapter 3. Progressive Dubiety: The Discontinuity of Disraeli's Political Trilogy

1. The catalyst for his adventures is his loss of his mistress's lock of hair. Although Disraeli is deliberately echoing *The Rape of the Lock* and is trying to connect Popanilla with the wit and wordliness of Alexander Pope, he does not maintain this urbanity. (That the first syllable of Popanilla's name contains Pope may be a naïve attempt to call attention to the parallel.)
2. Wolf, Introduction to the *The Young Duke*, p. xiv.
3. Blake, p. 171. Much of this paragraph is indebted to Blake's chapter VIII, entitled 'Young England'.
4. This 11 March 1842 letter to his wife is quoted by both Blake, p. 173, and Monypenny and Buckle, *The Life of Benjamin Disraeli, Earl of Beaconsfield*, II, p. 130.
5. The General Preface precedes *Lothair* in the Hughenden edition.

6. Steven Graubard, *Burke, Disraeli, and Churchill*, p. 115.
7. Quoted in Alice Chandler, *A Dream of Order* (Lincoln: University of Nebraska, 1970), p. 161.
8. See Sheila M. Smith, 'Willenhall and Wodgate: Disraeli's use of Blue Book Evidence', *Review of English Studies*, N.S. 13 (November, 1962), pp. 368–84; and Sheila M. Smith, 'Blue Books and Victorian Novelists', *Review of English Studies*, N.S. 21 (February, 1970), pp. 23–40.
9. George Eliot, *Scenes of Clerical Life*, Cabinet edition (Edinburgh: Blackwood and Sons, n.d.), pp. 162–3.
10. *The Letters of Disraeli to Lady Bradford and Lady Chesterfield*, 2 vols, ed Marquis of Zetland (New York: D. Appleton & Co., 1929), I, p. 372.
11. Blake, p. 265.
12. Blake, p. 202.
13. Disraeli, *Lord George Bentinck: A Political Biography*, p. 324.
14. Cecil Roth, *Benjamin Disraeli* (New York: Philosophical Library, 1952), p. 79.
15. See Blake, pp. 258–61.
16. Walter Houghton, *The Victorian Frame of Mind*, pp. 310, 330.
17. For an extensive discussion of similarities between Disraeli and Carlyle, see Morris Edmund Speare, *The Political Novel* (New York: Oxford University Press, 1924; reissued New York: Russell & Russell, 1966), pp. 170–1.
18. Preface to 1849 edition, reprinted as Note D in *Coningsby; or The New Generation*, ed. Bernard N. Langdon-Davis (New York: Capricorn, 1961), p. 587.
19. See Walter Houghton, *The Victorian Frame of Mind*, pp. 325–6.
20. Blake, p. 210.
21. Geoffrey H. Hartman, 'Romanticism and Anti-Self-Consciousness' in *Romanticism and Consciousness*, ed Harold Bloom (Norton: New York, 1970), p. 54.
22. Obvious examples are *Sartor Resartus, Apologia Pro Vita Sua* and *In Memoriam*. See Walter Houghton's *The Victorian Frame of Mind, 1830–1870* (New Haven and London: Yale University Press, 1957).
23. Elie Halevy, *Victorian Years 1841–1895*, trans E. I. Watkin (New York: Peter Smith, 1951), p. 62.
24. Richard A. Levine, *Benjamin Disraeli*, pp. 123–4. See pp. 114–20 of Levine's valuable study for an interesting discussion of how *Tancred* differs from *Sybil and Coningsby*. In *Disraeli*, Blake remarks that *Tancred* 'is the vehicle for Disraeli's own highly idiosyncratic views on race and religion' which 'have little connection with the ideas in *Coningsby* and *Sybil*' (p. 194). But Blake's observation, never fully explored, is directed toward the philosophy of the novels. My concern is also with the aesthetics of the political trilogy, and with how Disraeli's political views and psychological needs explain the shape and meaning of Disraeli's imagined worlds.
25. Levine, p. 124.
26. Hartman, p. 54.

Chapter 4. Art and Argument in 'Sybil'

1. Steven Graubard, *Burke, Disraeli, and Churchill*, p. 139.
2. Arnold Kettle, Raymond Williams, and Avrom Fleishman are notable exceptions.
3. Morris Edmund Speare, *The Political Novel*, pp. 170–1.

4. Robert Langbaum, *The Modern Spirit: Essays on the Continuity of Nineteenth and Twentieth Century Literature* (New York: Oxford University Press, 1970), p. 167.
5. Karl Marx and Friedrich Engels, *The Communist Manifesto*, orig. edn, 1849 (New York: Appleton-Century-Crofts, 1957, p. 33). For a penetrating comparison of Marx and Disraeli, see Sir Isaiah Berlin, 'Benjamin Disraeli, Karl Marx, and the Search for Identity'.
6. Elie Halevy, *The Triumph of Reform 1830–1841*, 2nd rev. edn, trans. E. I. Watkin (London: Ernest Benn 1950), p. 296.
7. R. W. Stewart, *Disraeli's Novels Reviewed*, p. 207.
8. R. W. Church, *The Oxford Movement*, reprinted (Chicago: University of Chicago Press, 1970), p. 250.
9. Blake, p. 171.
10. A. C. Chadwick, introduction to *The Mind of the Oxford Movement* (Stanford: Stanford University Press, 1960), p. 12.
11. One example from Coningsby will suffice: 'The custom of separating the sexes for [supper at balls], and arranging that the ladies should partake of it by themselves, though originally founded in a feeling of consideration and gallantry, and with the determination to secure, under all circumstances, the convenience and comfort of the fair sex, is really, in its appearance and its consequences, anything but European, and produces a scene which rather reminds one of the harem of a sultan than a hall of chivalry. To judge from the countenances of the favoured fair, they are not themselves particularly pleased; and when their repast is over, they necessarily return to empty halls, and are deprived of the dance at the very moment when they may feel most inclined to participate in its graceful excitement' (*Coningsby*, VI, viii, p. 340).
12. Quoted in A. C. Chandler, *A Dream of Order*, p. 167.
13. Arthur Frietzsche, *Disraeli's Religion*, Utah State University Monograph Series, Vol. 9, no. 1 (Logan: Utah University Press, 1961), p. 15.
14. See *Sybil* (V, v, p. 359) where Disraeli speaks of the 'insolence of the insignificant', when Sybil encounters *one* surly waiter as she is searching for her father.
15. Walter Houghton, *The Victorian Frame of Mind*, p. 343.
16. John Holloway, *The Victorian Sage* (New York: Macmillan, 1953), pp. 105, 106, 108. Richard Levine, *Benjamin Disraeli*, accurately observes '[Egremont] is far more successful as a theorizer and enunciator of political ideology than he is as a practical mover of political change' (p. 117).
17. See Sheila M. Smith, 'Willenhall and Wodgate: Disraeli's use of Blue Book Evidence', and her 'Blue Books and Victorian Novelists'.
18. Georg Lukaçs, *Studies in European Realism* (New York: Grosset & Dunlap, 1964), p. 12.

Chapter 5. The Argument and Significance of Disraeli's Last Novels

1. While the final novels have been given short shrift, there have been exceptions. Indeed, Robert Blake's *Disraeli* makes exaggerated claims for *Lothair*, regarding it as 'the best of all Disraeli's novels' (p. 518). Marius Bewley has praise for *Endymion*: 'The great trilogy of the 1840s, *Coningsby*, *Sybil*, and *Tancred*, and his last completed novel *Endymion* . . . exhibit a comprehensive engagement with

life on a very large stage, and a remarkable sympathy with it, to which Disraeli could only have come through his ardent lifelong pursuit of a political career'. ('Towards Reading Disraeli', *Prose* 4 [1972], 5–23). Yet Bewley's essay never again mentions *Endymion*. My discussion takes issue with John Holloway's implicit assumption that Disraeli's chronological development is immaterial. See his penetrating chapter on Disraeli in *The Victorian Sage* (New York: Macmillan, 1953).

2. Ian Gregor, Introduction to *Culture and Anarchy* (New York and Indianapolis: Bobbs-Merrill, 1971), p. xxxiv.
3. See Blake, chapter xxi, pp. 450–77.
4. *The Collected Works of Walter Bagehot*, ed. Norman St. John-Stevas, 9 vols (Cambridge, Massachusetts: Harvard University Press, 1968), III, p. 488. While our approaches and arguments differ, I agree with Bewley's contention that 'Disraeli's literary and political careers . . . are mutually corroborative of a personality that could not fully have expressed itself through either medium exploited solely in itself' ('Towards Reading Disraeli', p. 5).
5. Neither does the fragment *Falconet* on which Disraeli was working in his last months.
6. Monypenny and Buckle, *The Life of Benjamin Disraeli, Earl of Beaconsfield*, 6 vols, V, p. 149.
7. For a full account of these matters, see Blake, pp. 494–533, and Monypenny and Buckle, pp. 100–1.
8. Quoted in Monypenny and Buckle, IV, p. 362.
9. *Culture and Anarchy*, ed. Ian Gregor, pp. 111–13. Most of *Culture and Anarchy* was originally published as magazine articles in *Cornhill Magazine* between July 1867 and August 1868. See Gregor, p. xxxvi.
10. *Lord George Bentinck*, p. 320.
11. Lionel Trilling, *Mathew Arnold* (New York: Norton, 1939; reissued Meredian Press, 1955), p. 241.
12. *Culture and Anarchy*, ed. Ian Gregor, p. 31.
13. Ibid, pp. 149–50.
14. Ibid, pp. 39–40.
15. Ibid, p. 85.
16. Monypenny and Buckle, VI, p. 562.
17. Richard A. Levine, *Benjamin Disraeli*, p. 146.
18. James D. Merritt, 'The Novelist St. Barbe in Disraeli's *Endymion*: Revenge on Whom?' *Nineteenth-Century Fiction*, 23 (1968), 85–8. Merritt argues that St. Barbe satirises Carlyle as well as Thackeray.
19. Morris Edmund Speare, *The Political Novel*, p. 126.
20. Asa Briggs, *Victorian People*, p. 265.
21. Gertrude Himmelfarb, *Victorian Minds* (New York: Alfreda Knopf, 1968), p. 35–7.

Conclusion

1. Robert Blake, *Disraeli*, p. 175.
2. Charles Whibley, *Lord John Manner and his Friends*, 2 vols.; I, 148–9; quoted in Blake, p. 175.

Index